CHRONICLE

Childhood to Manhood

An Autobiography

STANLEY MASSEY

Published And Distributed By
New Dawn Publishing House
Los Angeles, California
Email: stanleymassey@yahoo.com

Packaging/Consulting
Professional Publishing House
1425 W. Manchester Ave. Ste B
Los Angeles, California 90047
323-750-3592
Email: professionalpublishinghouse@yahoo.com
www.Professionalpublishinghouse.com

Cover design: TWA Solutions
First printing April 2024
ISBN: 979-8-218-40568-7
10 9 8 7 6 5 4 3 2 1

Dedication

This book is dedicated to Love

Marie, Steven Jr. and Sam

TABLE OF CONTENTS

INTRODUCTION

This book serves as a testament to the life of a young African American male, chronicling his journey from childhood to adulthood. The narrative unfolds in chronological order, offering insight into the events that shaped his life at different stages.

During his early years, circumstances beyond his control influenced decisions and occurrences in his life. As time passed, he transitioned into making his own choices, some commendable, while others proved less wise. It became apparent to him that these decisions carried consequences, ultimately molding his character, prompting self-reflection, and fostering personal growth.

The journey involved enduring challenges, evolving perspectives, and a transformative shift in his thinking. The culmination of these experiences has contributed to the person he has become today.

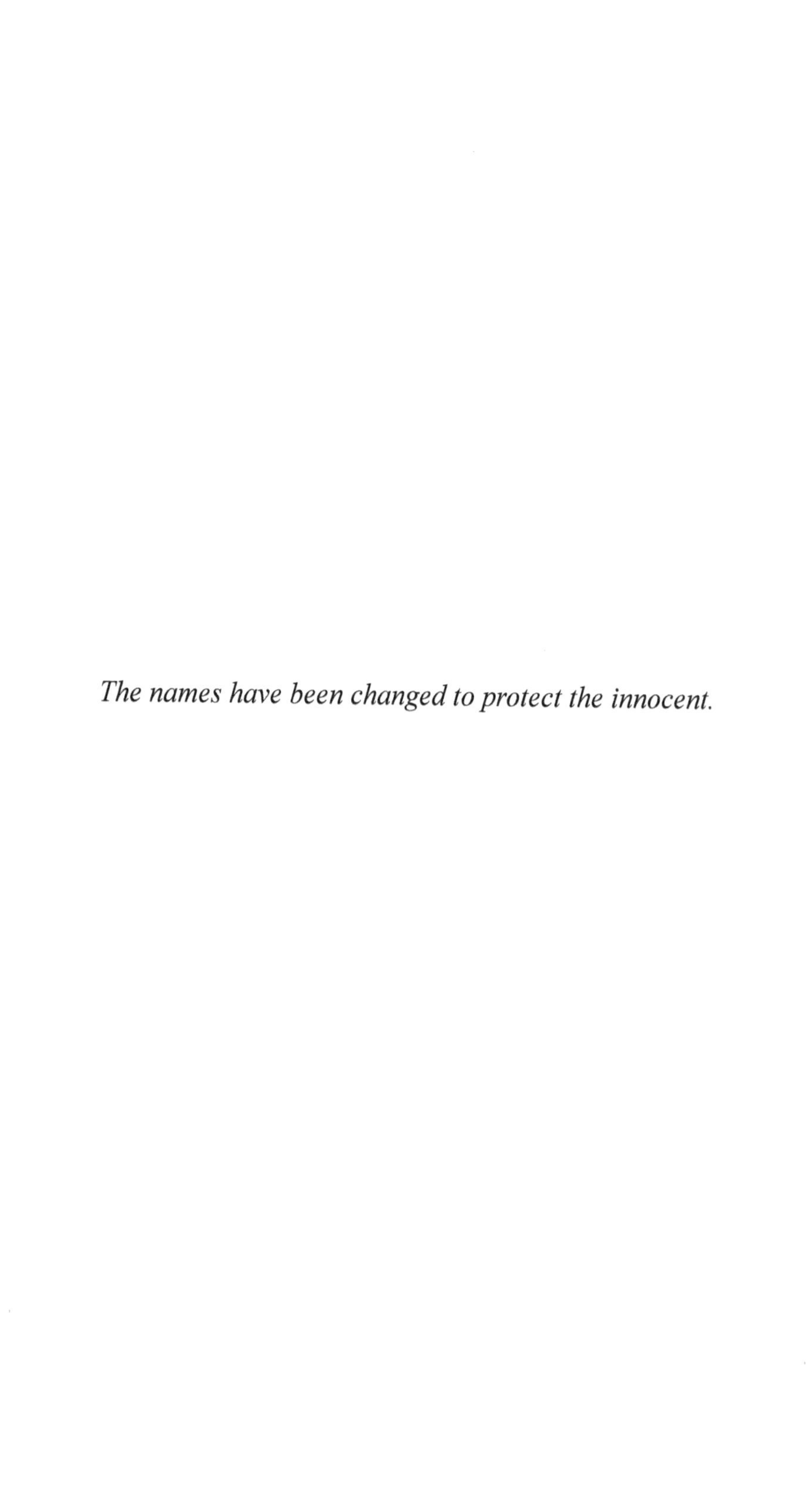

The names have been changed to protect the innocent.

CHAPTER 1

The Family

As a child of five years of age, I was eager to learn, energetic, and full of life. Unaware of what lay ahead, sheltered by a loving family life, was soon to open the eyes of this young Black boy. Born in South Philadelphia and forced to move to 1019 North Fourth Street, I had just begun living the life of a poor Black child. Not knowing the truth, I was already poor, Black, and just living. It was here when the doors of life opened, and the innocent became the product of a broken family.

There was my oldest sister, Debbie, my niece, Keysha, and her brother, Keith. Margaret was Keysha and Keith's mother and, from a child's understanding, Margaret was my mother as well. They called her Mom and so did I. I never heard Debbie call her "Mom." She always called her by her name. I thought because Debbie was older, she could do that. Besides, Margaret didn't seem to mind.

I was to start school next year, so Debbie spent a lot of time preparing me for that big day. Debbie was tall and thin, with a fair complexion and brown eyes. She took a special interest in being the one who would teach me what I needed to enter the first grade.

Debbie took me just about everywhere she went. When riding on the bus, she challenged me to spell things I saw from the bus window—the colors of cars, street names, stores, and shops. Debbie taught me very well, and I could tell she didn't mind teaching me.

Once, she asked me, "What color is glass?"

Every glass I looked at didn't have any color. "Glass has no color."

"Then it is clear."

"What does that mean?"

"You can see through it."

A new word to my vocabulary. Then she explained that some glass has color, but that would be another lesson. She answered any question, even the silly one-word questions like, "Why?" I didn't realize she was only in seventh grade. She had an answer to every question and seemed to know everything, and that amazed me. Patient, gentle, and very loving, she had a place in my heart that no one could ever have.

It was September 1965, and time for me to start school, but there was one problem. The school year started in September, and I would not be six until February 1966. Therefore, I had to wait another year. In Catholic school, you had to be six to start first grade. There was no kindergarten or preschool back in those days. I had one thought: I would be the only kid in first grade who turned seven before the end of the school year. What a drag; I would always be a grade behind or a year older than the other kids in my class. The wait was not a problem for Debbie, who used that time to teach me more of the things a kid my age should know. She taught me to read, write, and spell not only on a first-grade level but on the second- and third-grade level, too. She was more determined and driven to see me do well. What was her motivation? That was not a question for a kid to ask. I loved the attention and was happy to get it.

Well, that glorious day finally arrived, and the long wait was over. September 1966. It was my first day of school. Not knowing what I was truly in for, I was ready as can be, dressed in the school uniform—white shirt, navy blue clip-on tie with matching pants, and black shoes. Keysha and Debbie wore navy blue dresses that hung past their knees and had a patch on the left shoulder with the initials of the school's name on it. On the way to school, they tried to brief me on what to expect and how to behave once we arrived. I don't think I heard much of anything they said. Being nervous and excited at the same time was a little too much for me to handle at that age.

We turned the corner of the last block to walk to the school, Fifth and George Streets. There was a small ma-and-pa candy store on that corner. This made the corner special to most kids who passed it every day going to school. From this corner, I could see the giant cross on the top of the church. Now standing in front of Saint Peter's, I was in awe to see the size of the building. The bricks were not the small red bricks that made up my house. These were huge gray stones that appeared to weigh a ton and neatly stacked one on top of another. Once inside, there were long corridors with classrooms on both sides.

Kesha went into one room and said to me, "Be good."

Debbie and I continued down the long corridor. Toward the end, she said, "This is your classroom." Bending down to where I would be the only one to hear, she gave me my final instructions. Go in, take a seat, and wait for the teacher. My classroom is on the second floor." She kissed me, smiled, and walked away.

I entered the classroom with my head up, shoulders back, and a stride that said I had somewhere to go. I took a seat in the middle of the room and waited for the teacher, just as Debbie had said. With anticipation, I looked around the classroom. The rest of the kids had the same uniforms as I had on. I thought that was kind of funny because we all looked alike. The teacher's desk sat at the front of the room, taking up most of the front with a little room between it and the front row. Behind it was the blackboard made of slate—the stuff that gave you that eerie feeling when someone ran their fingernails across it—and trimmed in old-fashioned wood about two inches wide. It stretched from wall to wall and almost touched the ceiling. Above that were the alphabets in uppercase and lowercase letters. They were the largest letters I could ever remember seeing. The huge Big Ben clock with its little hand on the eight, the big hand a few dots before the twelve, and the long red second hand slowly creeping around. I had a few more minutes, so I continued to look around, turning my attention to the back of the room. The entire back wall was eight closet doors a few perfect inches apart. I could have only imagined what could be in them. They weren't big, and it didn't appear they could hold much. I thought maybe they were used to locking the bad kids in.

Startled by the bell, I turned around to see the kids scrambling to their seats. In a split second, they were all seated at attention and quiet, as though not breathing. Then, something covered from head to toe in all-black, barely exposing the eyes, nose, and mouth, entered the room and sat behind the enormous desk in the front. Suddenly, I heard nothing outside my body. I could only hear my heart beating like a bass drum inside my head and the rapid flow of blood shooting through my veins. From the sight of this thing, I felt warm all over. My eyes were now the size of silver dollars, and, along with my scrambled thoughts, I was overwhelmed with fear. I immediately jumped to my feet and ran out of the room, screaming at the top of my lungs.

"Debbie! Debbie!" I yelled as I dashed down the hall and made my way up the stairs. I hit those stairs, skipping two and three steps at a time.

I turned on the first landing, never looking back, yelling for Debbie all the while. The second landing came quickly, and I was through the door, down another hall with classrooms on both sides. I stuck my head in each room and scanned the faces with bulging eyes, noticing all the students looked just as frightened as me. In each room, behind the enormous desk, was another object covered in black. It scared the students so badly that they all sat motionless, not even daring to breathe. I continued my search down the hall, entering one room after another, screaming her name. Finally, halfway down the hall, I peered into a room and saw a face I recognized seated in the center. I called out to her, and she ran to meet me at the door. She grabbed me, and I held on for dear life. Her words were soft but quick. "What's wrong?" I looked up at her, tears streaming down my face, while pointing with a trembling finger toward the thing covered in black.

She smiled her warm and gentle smile and wiped the tears from my face. She kissed my forehead while holding my cheeks and said, "That is the teacher."

Debbie walked me toward the figure, and as we got closer, I could see it was a person. Debbie held my hand and introduced me to her teacher. "This is my baby brother, and today is his first day at school."

The teacher spoke with a voice just as soft as Debbie's, saying it was okay and nodding.

Debbie asked to be excused so she could walk me back to my class. On the way, she explained, "They are called nuns or sisters, and that is the way they dress." She reassured me, "The nuns will not hurt you. They will teach you all the things you need to know to get through school."

When we arrived at my classroom, Debbie asked, "Are you all right now?"

I said, "Yes."

We entered the class. She pointed to my seat, and I sat down.

Debbie and the teacher talked for a minute, then Debbie looked at me with another reassuring smile and left the room.

My first day of school, what a disaster. Excited to be here and scared to death of the thing they called a nun.

It didn't take long to get used to the idea of going to school daily. Eventually, it became a way of life. Besides, it appeared this was the life of kids. I mean, what else could we have done?

The teacher noticed I was a good student. I did as I was told, completed all my work, and was quick about doing it. It all seemed too easy. Debbie's teaching truly prepared me for this school year. Reading, writing, counting, and spelling all fell into place, and I owed it all to Debbie, the best teacher of all time.

One day, like any other day, I was sitting at my desk doing my work when the nun called my name.

"Steven, will you come here, please?"

I could not imagine what the "thing," I mean, the nun wanted me for. I did nothing wrong, nor was I talking to anyone. "What does she want?" was all I could ask myself as I walked toward her sitting behind that enormous desk.

"Do you know who your mother is?"

I stood before her in awe. I thought that was a dumb question to ask. Every kid knew their mother. "Yes."

She looked me in the eyes. "Then tell me, who is your mother?"

That's how they did it, to see if you were going to tell the truth if you knew what you were talking about. They looked into your eyes as if they were looking into your soul.

This angered me. So, for a moment, I stared back into her blue eyes, searching for the reason for the question. Then, I gave her a stern face and a voice to match. "My mother's name is Margaret Mathews."

"Margaret is your sister and Keysha and Keith are her children."

For a moment, the world had stopped moving, and I was spinning. The questions raced through my head. Who was this person, sitting before me, telling me who my mother was?

How in the world would she know? She definitely was not a part of my family.

"The school records that Margaret submitted indicate that she is your sister."

It was a lightning bolt through my heart to hear those words and I felt my heart melt like wax from a candle. Without saying a word, I turned and walked furiously to my seat.

I sat there looking down at my desk, eyes full of water, head full of confusion. To a child, Mom was God, and I wasn't sure I had one either. Not comprehending anything that was going on in the classroom, I wanted the day to end so I could go home. I could not wait for that two-thirty bell. When I looked at the clock, the little hand was at the two, the big hand was one tick from the six and the second hand crept toward the twelve. When the bell sounded, I leaped to my feet, darted to the door, and ran down the hallway, passing everyone and never looking behind to see the trail I had left. I ran past Debbie and Keysha at the front gate. Nothing to be said. I became my favorite cartoon hero, the Flash. The sound of the wind whistled in my ears; my tie waved in the wind as I dashed down the street toward home. No time to waste. I was stopping for nothing and no one, only to look for cars before crossing the street. I was the Flash, the fastest man on Earth. Cars were my least of worries.

Mom

The house came into sight, and my feet moved faster, as though not touching the ground. Skipping the few steps in front of the house, I turned the knob and dashed through the door, standing in the living room. My heart pounded like a drum, and my lungs burned for lack of air as I hollered for the person dearest to me. "Mom!"

She came running down the stairs. At the sight of her baby boy standing in the center of the room with tears in his eyes, she stopped on the staircase. "What's wrong?"

"Are you my mother?" That was the question of the year.

Her heart shattered like a crystal thrown to the ground. Her lips quivered as she tried to answer in a sincere voice. Her eyes filled with tears as the word "Yes" rolled off her tongue. She continued down the stairs, ran to her wounded child, and threw her around me tightly. On her knees, she whispered in my ear those words to reassure me. "Yes ,I'm your mother. I am the only mother you will ever have."

Locked in each other's arms, tears streaming down our faces, mother and son sobbed together for a moment.

As Margaret slowly released me and sat me on the sofa, she told me the true story of my existence. "I am your sister. There are three more girls and four more boys who are your brothers and sisters."

Wiping the tears from her face, she named the others in order, starting from the oldest down to me: Lewis, Eric, herself (Margaret), Stephanie, Cynthia, Ray, Debbie, Mark, and me (Steven). Most of these names I did not recognize.

"Shortly after you were born, Mommy died, and Mommy's sister, Loretta, came to divide the family. Lewis and Eric were of age, so she took all the others in between and left you behind. I claimed you as my son along with my two kids, Kesha and Keith, to prevent the social service people from taking you away. Our father, Henry, was never around, so he could do nothing to prevent the family from being split apart. I don't think he really cared."

I sat there quietly, unsure of what was next. This was a lot for a kid my age to handle. I rose from the sofa, walked the stairs in complete silence, and went to my bedroom to change my school clothes. I was numb. All of what I used to feel had left my body. It was as though someone or something had reached deep inside me and took my spirit away. The loving, energetic little boy was now lost within himself, with one thought never to allow feelings like these to affect him ever again. How could I explain the hurt or the pain? It was emptiness, total darkness; it was truly being alone.

Aunt Loretta

I continued to do well in school and, to a degree, was happy with what I was doing. But it wasn't long before I went through a major change, this one much worse than the first. It came before I had reached the second grade. My aunt Loretta came to the house to inform my sister, Margaret, who I call Mom, that there was no need for her to continue to raise me. Afterwards, there was this big family talk of my aunt coming to get me to live with her. Why, suddenly, would Aunt Loretta want to get me to live with her? The family said it could be for the money. I did not know that the government gave money to people who had to raise children. Loretta had the rest of my brothers and sisters in her care already, so why me? Why now? The family said it could have only been one reason: money. I would bring more money to her household if I was in her custody.

At seven years old, I was living with her, and I did not know what to expect. It took a short time to find out that life with Aunt Loretta would be very hard. Right away, she was strict and mean to me. I also was with my siblings: Ray, Mark, Debbie, Stephanie, and Cynthia. For the first time, I now realized that these were my brothers and sister. As I remembered Stephanie and Cynthia were in the house for a short time. It was not long before they both had gotten married, and they held their weddings in the house. By the time I had reached third grade, Loretta was the wicked witch of Orianna Street.

She made us clean the house every day and there was always something to scrub, dust, wipe down, or clean. No mops were in the house at all. I became her primary target. It seemed as though she took all her anger out on me. Mark became her pet. This was because one day when she was beating him something fierce, he hid a hatchet under the old roller washer machine. He allowed her to beat him to where he reached under the washer, pulled out the hatchet, and threatened to chop her head off. He told her that if she ever laid another hand on him, he would kill her. You should have seen her frozen in place, mouth open, probably not knowing if he would do it or not. I don't know if he would do it or not either, but she never laid another hand on Mark again, at least not to beat him.

I was the darkest in complexion of the family as far as those who lived in the house, but I did not care about those things. I did not see us as light skin or dark skin. All I knew was we were a family; brothers and sisters. I spent much of my time with Laureta. When she went shopping, I was with her. When she was cooking, I was there to set the table and to bring what she needed to prepare the food. If not that, I would sit at the table reading books while she was cooking. I was not out of the house very much alone or for very long. When my chores were done, I was still by her side, helping around the house or in the yard and in the garden.

Friends who knew us or who were allowed inside the house used to say that we had the cleanest house on the block. Our house even had a name by those who knew us well. They called our house the "house of correction." Loretta taught me everything from that point on—cooking, her way of cleaning the house, and the proper way to weed the garden for better plant growth. I had to learn how to sew and hem my pants. She taught me to wash my white shirts by hand and scrub the collar, hang them to line dry, and press them with perfect sleeve creases. She kept me reading books, so I could read in school. There was always the finest teaching of all. She kept me in order and how to obey her—a lesson I learned very well. Her famous words were: I could only speak when I've been spoken to. It was either learning it or getting beaten. There was no choice as a child, even though she would beat me pretty often. There were some things that took a while to learn, so the results of that was a beating. There was always something for me to do. I was busy constantly.

When I did something wrong, the beatings were severe and painful. She would throw two pennies on the floor and say, "Your father doesn't give me two red pennies for you." I truly think she used to beat me for that fact, not that I'd actually done something wrong. I was never clean enough for her; my skin was always dirty, and I never cleaned myself well enough for her. So, this was her reason for giving me a bath and scrubbing me with scrub brushes. She would scrub my knees and elbows so fiercely that when I got out of the tub, I felt like I was on fire. She convinced me how dirty I was by making me wipe my skin with cotton soaked with rubbing alcohol and, of course, it would come up dirty each time. I didn't know that was skin on the cotton.

I became withdrawn, quiet, and closed. I talked less and less to the family or when anyone was around. I didn't want to be anywhere she was because, for me, it meant trouble. Nothing I did was ever good enough for her. It could always be better, and she always had a better way of doing everything. Her way was the best. I don't remember too many times when she rewarded me with a hug or a kiss. She rarely showed any of those emotions or acts of affection toward me. Something so common between a child and a parent was far and few, if any at all, between us. I never heard those common words that would accompany that hug and kiss. Those three little words that could make your heart leap or bring tears to your eyes. No, I never heard them, never. Not from her. "I love you." I never got that from her. It is strange to imagine that in all this, she was everything to me. I could do nothing without her permission. I woke up to her voice; my entire day centered on her. What she thought of me and everything I did was the weight I carried on my mind every day. Even at school, I worried about doing the right thing because she was the long arm of the law, and she could reach me anywhere from any place and at any time.

I was an honor roll student in Catholic school and seldom got into trouble. I knew to do well, or I would get beat well once I got home. I began hating her. I didn't like the way she looked or what she did. I didn't like the sound of her voice. I didn't want to be anywhere around her. She became the monster in my life. Most children's monsters were in the closet, under the bed, or shadows in the dark. My monster walked around during the day, sat at the table, had access to the entire house, and that was very frightening. I went into myself, not knowing what that was. My thoughts were the safe place in my head. I stopped talking and only spoke when and if I had something to say, which was hardly ever. That saying, "A child should be seen and not heard," was only partly true in my case. I was not seen and I had better not make any noise. There were no other children in the house, so I became invisible.

Everything was a lesson to learn. She taught me to always read, to study, and to be strong. The lessons went into the summer when school was out for most kids. I was in school in the house. Things got much worse around the house. It was never clean enough. I was never right enough, and I could never get beat enough.

Loretta was going through that thing that women her age go through—menopause. It was on her, and I felt its sting every day. No one knew what was wrong. We thought those were her ways, and we accepted it. The change of life is nothing to play with. It will sneak up on you gradually and once you are in its grip, it is so hard to overcome. My brother, Ray, spent most of his time away from the house. He was working and had a car, but although he was about eighteen, she would try to beat him still. Mark was away in the Marines. Debbie was growing as a young woman and she did not allow my aunt to touch her at all. Debbie stood her ground and watched over me more. Because everyone was out of the house, most of the time I was there to get my ass beat two or three times a day.

For the next two or three years, that was the norm for me. We were under her roof, which meant her rules and her direction. She ran the house, and all that was in it. I continued to do exceptionally well in school and made the honor roll. It felt great to be recognized as a person even if it only came from just other kids.

I remember the spelling contest. The girls against the boys was how it usually played out. I was the last boy standing and Janet was, for the most part, the last girl. It was fun but when one of us lost to the other, it put a little strain on our friendship. As kids, we both knew early that teachers and parents pushed us, and that push was the reason to end in a draw. School, with all the parts I disliked, was a place that I could be a kid or just be me, but never and I mean never too free.

By the time I reached eleven years old, there was talk of skipping me to a higher grade level. I was already reading and writing at that level. But of course, it had to be my aunt's final decision. You would have thought she would be happy for me, or at least proud. None the less, when the school suggested promoting me up one grade, she said no. She gave this lame-ass reason that I needed to grow up with the kids my age. Hell, she hardly ever let me out of the damn house. How was I to grow up with kids, let alone kids my age.

I can't say life was all that bad then. Besides, that life was all I knew. How was I to know it could be better? My next to the oldest brother would show me that there was much more to life than I had ever imagined. Eric would come by, pick me up, and take me to the lake, amusement parks, and to the park for picnics. It was freedom like I could have never imagined and the best part of it all was my aunt Loretta was not there with us. I think she would try to compete with my brother once in a while by taking me to a movie. It would never compare to the time and fun I had when I was with my brother. The one factor that meant so much to me was that she would not be there. She just did not understand that, and I could never tell her either.

For what I knew about life, it seemed okay. I had all I needed: a place to live, food, clothes, brothers, and sisters and I can't leave out those ass whippings. I did not have a reason to feel deprived. From my understanding, I had it all. But there were many times when I felt God, the little I knew of God, was punishing me. For what? For the life of me, I could not figure it out. I became angry. Not at God, but at the situation with my aunt. I got angry and angrier—so angry that family members would say I was mean and evil. I closed up completely. I would not talk because I had nothing to say. I would not ask questions. Why would I ask questions when the answers were not anything I wanted to hear? I just did what I was told, and I did it without speaking a word.

Now entering the sixth grade, the house got very empty most of the time. My brothers were always gone or out doing what growing teenagers did. Chasing girls was the thing, and I saw some of that when my brothers would sneak them in the basement from time to time. I would hide in the shadow or behind the furnace. My brother would beg the girls for something, but most of the time, she would say no. My sister, Debbie, was the only girl left at home, but she was the attention of the boys in the neighborhood. She must have been around seventeen or eighteen and caught the eye of all the guys. There were still many things going on within the fabric of the family, but they kept much of it away from me. I guess they still saw me as too young for grown-up matters.

One day after school, I came home to find the front door unlocked. I could see the latch was barely showing. I thought, *Why is the door open?* I slowly pushed the door and entered the house, closing the door behind me quietly. I said nothing, nor did I yell out. I never did that anyway. The house was very quiet and still. There was no smell of food cooking in the kitchen. I walked into the dining room and then into the kitchen to the table.

My brother, Mark, was on the floor, as if asleep. He only had one shoe on and the foot without a sock and the shoe had a hypodermic needle stuck in it. He looked asleep, but he might have been dead. I dropped my books, turned, and ran toward the front door. Once at the door, I realized he may need help. He could be dead. Where was I going? My mind raced uncontrollably, and my hands and knees shook the same. I stopped, turned toward the kitchen and walked back in that direction with a steady and careful pace. When I reached my brother, I said in a low voice, "Oh shit." I took the needle out of his foot and wrapped it in paper and put in the trashcan in the small kitchen. I leaned over him to see if he was still alive, but I could not tell. So, I stooped down, placed one hand on his chest, and put my face close to his nose. I could feel his breath on my lips as his chest rose and fell slowly. To make sure he was alive, I held his nose for a couple of seconds, and he opened his mouth for air. At that moment, I knew he was not dead.

I called his name a few times, but he never responded. I had to get him upstairs before anyone got home. I put on his sock and sneaker but did not tie it. Then I hoisted him up into a sitting position and got him to his feet. I struggled to get him to lean on my back, but did so, knowing this would be the only way I could get him up the stairs. I dragged him to the first set of stairs and began the climb. Midway up the stairs, I was straining and breathing heavily. Once on the landing of the second floor, the true definition of dead weight became a reality. It was heavy, hard to control, and it got heavier with every step. The second-floor stairs were narrower, with a sharp curve that almost made it impossible for both of us to get around. I got him to stand on the stairs when we neared the top and I pushed him up to the floor level. Then I went up and pulled him into bed, where he fell motionless. After putting his feet on the bed, I covered him with a blanket and went downstairs. I looked around the kitchen to make sure everything was in order. I picked up my books and placed them on the table and straightened the chairs that were out of place. I got a glass of water and sat down to do my homework, or at least try to.

Soon, the rest of the family began coming home. My brother, Ray, asked how long I had been home by myself. I told him I wasn't alone. Mark was upstairs asleep. There was nothing to say about what had just taken place.

When Mark awoke, I was by his side. He asked, "How did I get upstairs and in bed."

I said, "I did it."

He smiled and said, "Thanks."

There was nothing else to say. He knew I had taken care of everything. Neither of us mentioned it to the family. Mark and I never talked about it, so it was forgotten.

Loretta's mid-life crisis got worse. She showed signs of insanity. She was never a drinker, so I can honestly say it was not her drinking. If and when she had a drink, it would only be one glass of beer. A quart of beer would last her a whole week unless someone else drank it. I saw how things affected her, things she could not control or even explain. She took more baths during the day, sometimes three or four. This may not sound strange to you, but she would scrub herself so hard that her skin would welt and turn red as fire. At this, she would say to me, "You can never be clean enough." There were other odd things that she did, but I just thought this was her normal way of behaving. She was always eccentric. She became quiet and off to herself. I mean, it was only she and I in the house most of the time. I would peek around walls and in other rooms to see her standing in the middle of the room as if she had lost something, was thinking, maybe forgot something or just contemplating. She became lost in her own thinking. I didn't understand it. I was much too young still.

I watched her with a careful eye. I saw something was wrong, but I could not identify it and it was even harder to explain. Now, instead of her watching over me, I was the one watching over her. I would be in a room listening for her voice, a noise, or just any sound. There were long periods of time when there was nothing. I would peek in and she would be there alone, quiet and in thought. In my heart, it hurt me to see her this way. I couldn't explain that either.

One day, I came home from school, knocked on the door, she answered and said, "What are you doing home?"

I walked in and said, "School is out, and this is the time I usually get home, and it is three o'clock. If you don't believe me, you can call the time." I must have been out of my mind to talk to her that way. If she wasn't sick, this would tell me. Any other time, she would have beat me for days for that tone of voice and those words.

Instead, she just looked over her glasses and said, "The time is wrong," then she opened the door and told me to go back to school.

I left the house, but I did not go back to school. There would be no one there. I went to a small playground and played some basketball for about an hour. Something was wrong, but what could it be to make her act this way?

After an hour or so of playing, I had to get home. I still had all this and other things on my mind. I was now afraid to go home because it was one hour past the usual time I got in from school. All the way home, I could not think straight. The thoughts were racing through my mind. I couldn't figure out what she was up to. What did she mean when she said the time was wrong? From my understanding, when you called the time, they were never wrong. I knew one thing for sure: I was going to get a beating, no doubt about that. I did not know she was as sick as she was. By this time, she was in full bloom of mid-life crisis. She was deep in that stage of menopause that made some women go insane. But as a kid, I did not know that. I just didn't understand why she did the things she did or why she did them to me? Still, I was an hour late, and I had no explanation. I ran to shorten the time. My heart was pounding like a bass drum. The sweat rolled off my forehead and into my eyes by the glassful. My lungs were on fire from the heavy breathing. My entire body trembled as I tried to compose myself before knocking on the door. This was fear. I had never been this afraid before. Loretta opened the door and said, "Go change your clothes and come to the kitchen with your books."

I walked in and was shocked that she did not mention a word about what time it was or how late I was. On my way upstairs, I heard her in the kitchen singing and I smelled the aroma of great food that filled the entire house. It was rare to hear her sing, and it was also a treat. There is nothing like the sound of a woman singing, a wonderful sign of happiness. I returned to the kitchen table with my books and instructions for homework. She was not angry, nor was she upset; she was not mean. She was just peaceful, and I liked it. I can't remember ever seeing her like this. Little did I know that this would be the last time I would see her in such a happy mood.

CHAPTER 2

Loretta Leaving

One day after school, I came home to find Loretta packing a large dark green Army duffel bag. As I entered her bedroom, she had her clothes neatly folded on the bed. The Army bag was half full as she continued carefully placing the folded clothes in it.

I asked, "Are we going somewhere?"

It was she and I in the house and if she were leaving, I knew she was taking me.

She answered without raising her head and without looking at me. "No, you can't go this time." Her voice was soft and calm. She continued to pack the bag without looking up. When she finished, she pulled the strings tight, snapped a buckle to secure the bag, hoisted it over her shoulder, and headed down the stairs. I followed, neither of us talking, but I was thinking, *I know she will not leave me in this big old house all by myself. I'm going, too.* Loretta opened the door, and, still not convinced that I was not going, I stayed close behind her and she knew I was there. She stepped out the door and turned so that I was still standing in the doorway. She bent down to my level, placed her hand on my left cheek, and said, "You can't go, baby."

I looked into her eyes as she looked into mine. What seemed an eternity was merely a few seconds. My heart fell to a beat so slowly I could not hear it or feel it. I wondered if she felt it, too. She never called me baby. She turned and walked away, positioning the bag on her shoulder, leaving me frozen in time and in space. That feeling came over me again, that feeling of fear. Once again, I realized I was all alone. Another person was walking out of my life, leaving me behind.

Loretta walked to the corner of Orianna and Callaway Streets, where the old cardboard box company stood. The building was about five stories high, red brick, with many windows and a few enormous doors for shipping and receiving. It was there she placed her bag against the wall and paced the sidewalk. I could still see her with her hat tilted to the side just as the Green Beret soldiers wore theirs.

It must have been spring because it rained a light drizzle. The light from the sun allowed her to remain seen by this kid, who now felt that lonely feeling in his heart. But although I felt it for her and not myself, I remained tearless. It would be at least two to three hours before anyone would come home so I could tell them what had happened. As she paced the sidewalk, I paced the living room floor. Every so often, I would look outside and could still see her pacing in the same area, pacing. She was unsure of where to go. She was thinking of what to do next. These were my thoughts as I tried to read her mind. I sat in the living room, trying to figure things out. She was lost and needed help. I went to call my older sister Margret. As I ran to the phone, I thought, *What if she leaves?* I ran to the door to see if she was still there. She was gone. The bag was gone, too. It had stopped raining but her last words to me were to stay here. I'd always done what I was told, so I remained in the house until someone came home.

Finally, my brother, Ray, came home, and I was excited to see him. I shot words at him like a machine gun.

"Slow down," he said. "What are you talking about?"

I gathered my words and said, "Loretta is gone. She left. She was pacing back and forth in front of the box factory and now she is gone."

"So, good."

"What do you mean? Go get her. You need to go find her."

He pushed me aside. "She'll come home sooner or later."

Shortly after, Debbie came home, and I knew she would listen. I told her what had happened, and she listened without interrupting.

She said, "Don't worry. I will take care of you. It will be all right."

Debbie was true to her word. She took care of me, the house, and all that came with it, kept me fed, got me to school on time, and kept my grades up. She helped with my homework and studying for tests, gave me chores, and allowed me to go out to play. It was a treat to go outside. As time went on, I would ask, "Where is Loretta?"

Debbie would tell me in a soft voice, "I really don't know, but I will do all I can to find her."

In those moments, we both realized one thing: our aunt may have been strict, but we both cared for her in our own way. My sister was gentle with me, kind and loving in a motherly kind of way. I liked this and wanted it to last forever. Debbie must have figured out the possibility of Loretta never coming home again. So, without my knowing, she asked the family to help take care of me. How did I come to know she was asking for help? The day came when she asked if I would like to live with my other sister, Stephanie. I did not have to answer. She knew I did not want to leave her side.

Life with Debbie was wonderful to me. She had taught me to dance and how to hold a girl while dancing, shared in my excitement when I did well in school, never allowed me to stray from the pattern of school and chores, and hugged, kissed, and told me she loved me. Why in the world would I want to give that up? She was the best part of my life.

Debbie gave me all the reasons it would be best for me to live with our sister and her young family. She told me that Stephanie had kids I could grow up with; Stephanie was married, and it would be good for me to live with a man around the house. I did not care about any of that stuff. I never had it before, so what was the big deal now? She would bring up the conversation from time to time throughout the school year. I would ignore it and go on with what I was doing. She was always so gentle with me and never did much to upset me. I liked that about her. The end of the school year came, and little did I know, they had already decided for me. I would have to leave Debbie to live with Stephanie and her family.

Debbie told me that the family had decided that it would be best for me to live with Stephanie. I thought the family never decided anything for me, so why now? Where were they and their big decision-making power when I was getting all those ass-whippings? The time came when she sat me down for a long talk. She asked me to remember how good it would be for me to be around other kids. Then she eased the conversation more to the truth at hand. She told me she could no longer take care of me. She spoke of legal complications as if I understood. Some of those complications involved financial stress. Money was a huge factor in family matters in those days. She then said, "The bottom line is, you have to leave."

I heard those words so plainly—daggers through a child's heart. With tears in my eyes, I said, "I won't be a problem and I won't cost much. I don't need any money and you won't need money to take care of me." Again, I heard the words that pushed the knife ever so deeper through my heart and soul.

"You have to go." She hugged and kissed the tears that ran slowly down my cheeks, telling me all the good things that would occur while living with Stephanie. She told me Stephanie could afford to have me there and also she would love for me to be there. She told me the benefits of having Stephanie's husband as my brother-in-law, but more importantly as a father image. It all made sense. I understood it all, but that did not ease the pain of knowing I would have to leave. Everything inside of me said something different. One more time, I would be alone. They really did not want me and again I was being sent away.

Packing was easy. I had little. All that belonged to me fit in a bag or two. The twenty-five-minute walk was in complete silence. What was to be said? Better yet, I didn't care.

I was thirteen, in the seventh grade, and living with Stephanie and her family. They handed me a key to the house, along with a list of responsibilities. They gave me a curfew, which did not make any sense at all to me. I had never been out of the house alone after dark. I had a bedroom of my own, and chores like washing the dishes three or four times a week, cleaning the bathroom, and putting out the trash. It was always understood. It went without saying. I, of course, had to keep up my grades in school. But they said it anyway.

"You know you better keep up with your school grades or you will lose all the privileges."

I had one question about that. "Is it a privilege to wash the dishes, clean the bathroom, and put out the trash?" Although in my mind I dared not ask, I was smarter than that. I guess it would be okay living here. It would have to be. I had no other choice.

Eric would come by once in a while to visit my sister and her family. Eric was the second oldest of the family of brothers and sisters. I didn't see much of him, but while out riding my bike, I might catch him at a local watering hole. Although I was way too young to be in a bar, it was okay because everyone knew my brother and I would be with him. He would ask a few questions about my life, but never would he get involved. I might have gotten a beer out of him, but just one, and it would be one of those small nips or a Rolling Rock. He advised me to always be good and to go straight home no matter the time.

I continued to do well in school, and I liked the attention I got when people thought of me as being smart. I never cared about the other kids' grades. I knew I had to keep mine up or else. I was now in the eighth grade and excitement was in the air. My grades were good, and the potential was even better. The potential was so great that one of my sisters told me that my mom died for a reason and that it was for me to make the family proud. Was I to think my mother died so I could make the family proud? I don't think so. There weren't many who graduated or even went to high school. The family kept telling me I had a good chance to go anywhere I wanted to go to high school. In Catholic school, students graduated from eighth grade to ninth grade, and ninth through twelfth was high school. There was no junior high that I knew of.

My sisters had a lot of confidence in me. They would tell me I was smart, and that I was going to be something someday. I used to wonder what that something was. Cynthia would sit down once in a while and have long talks with me about the way it used to be. She told me about life with our mother and how hard things were. She spoke of a time I could not remember, although I thought these times were just as hard. Cynthia felt she and I were the outcasts of the family. She used to say they treated us differently. I just thought that was just the way it was. She never had to say directly or exactly what that treatment was, but within our minds and hearts, we both knew. There was never much talk about our mother as far as what she looked like, her hair, eyes, or the way she walked or talked, and I knew not to ask. I was always told I was a baby when she died, and the family had no pictures.

Cynthia had one item that she said belonged to my mother. She took me upstairs to her bedroom and told me to sit on the end of the bed. She went into the closet, pulled down a box, and said, "This is the only thing that is left of Mommy's."

I asked, "What is it?"

"Open it."

When I did, it was a silk or satin slip, a half-slip women wore under their garments. I pressed it against my face and took a deep breath. It had an old but good clean smell to it. My sister left the room. The tears began to fall and roll ever so slowly down my cheeks. Something rose from within my heart. It was huge, but what? I was crying and didn't know why.

Cynthia came back into the bedroom and asked, "Are you all right?"

I didn't respond.

"I thought it was time and you are old enough to handle it," she said. She then asked if I wanted the slip.

"No, you better keep it. You have had it all this time; almost seventeen years."

She took it from me, folded it neatly, and placed it into the box. Cynthia told me that whenever I wanted it or needed to see it, all I had to do was ask.

I nodded and said, "Okay."

It's not that I did not want it, but what was I going to do with it? It could not bring my mother back, and I had no memories of her. I know this; I had four sisters, and, to me, they were my mothers. Try living with that.

The eighth-grade school year was coming to an end and preparation for graduation had begun. Stephanie was there to give her support and said whatever I wanted to wear, she would buy it for me. Graduation came and went just as fast.

My sister had most of the family at her house for the occasion, and it was nice to see us all together. I had made the honor roll, and that really made the family proud. Stephanie had gotten me this huge card and had everyone fill it with money. She had a way of getting us together and keeping us that way. I remember she used to say, "If you don't have family, you don't have anything."

I started studying for the entry exam at one of the best high schools in the city. I wanted to go the Saint John's Prep—known as the Prep because of its strict rules and required academics. The test was long and hard, but I took it just to see if the Prep was for me. My sister was a little concerned and asked if I had a second choice for high school, and I did. When the results came in, I had missed the entry qualifications by one point. It was another thing that made me question where we lived and the things that shaped how we lived. You reject a kid from entering your school program because he missed the entry exam by one point.

Stephanie had some good words to comfort me. "Sometimes you tend to push yourself to the extreme and you may need to slow down once in a while."

"All I know is to do my best, or at least try."

"I know, Steve." I could see she also understood.

Well, I did not make the Prep, so it was off to Roman Catholic. There were about three hundred freshmen that year and only sixty to seventy-five of them were Black. By the first report, I had made the honor roll, but it was not the same. I had more freedom after school and hung out and did what teenage boys did. We thought it was harmless to, once in a while, drink beer and smoke weed. I had to keep it from the family while I continued to make good grades. I asked my sister if I would be able to leave Catholic school by my tenth-grade year. I also learned more about the street life and how it worked. I saw that life was not all of what they taught in Catholic school. Life in the streets was sad and scary. Stephanie said I could change schools if I kept my grades up and when I went to public school, I would have to do the same there.

I had to move on because Catholic school was not all it was made out to be. On the outside, it was a fine education, but on the inside, it was rigorous discipline and intense studying. I remember seeing a priest smack a kid in the face and I thought to myself, *No one ever taught that kid to defend himself.* The trouble I got in was mostly questions I had about real life that were contrary to what I learned in school. I became interested in the street life. I was learning about my people, Black people, and where we came from. I saw where we were in society, where we did not fit in a white society. I saw how many of us were poor, my family included. I saw how people treated us and how they did not respect us as individuals. I felt a new kind of hurt, one of anger, rebellion, and sorrow. I saw the misfortune of the Black race, and I blamed it on the white race. I believe they caused all our problems. I believed they were the monsters in our lives, and they caused our poverty. I questioned the priests and what they taught. This kind of questioning got the interest of some of the faculty, and they would have me remain after school to question me on where I was learning what I knew.

I had to call my brother-in-law, Tom, to pick me up from school a couple of times. He asked, "What seemed to be the reason for them to question what you are learning? You make good grades."

I told him, "I questioned them about the color of the God they teach us about. If He is Spirit, then He has no color. It says do not worship idles, and they make me face statues of all kinds and pray to them. Aren't these statues considered idles?

Tom suggested maybe it was time for me to go to a public school just to see what or how the learning process was in the public school system and to be around more kids of my own race.

By the end of the ninth-grade year, my grades were good enough for me to convince my sister that I would continue to do the same in a public school. By the end of my freshman year at Roman Catholic, I had the third-best report of that freshman class. It was a good feeling, but it felt better knowing that I would go to a public school the following year.

I was at the age where I was becoming interested in girls. I noticed their walk, shape, and how they developed all over.

I went to my sister Debbie to get answers on which I was unclear. She explained love is what a husband and wife have. Sex is what a girlfriend and boyfriend do, and children are the results in both cases. She still was my best teacher. During that time, I had a Puerto Rican girlfriend. We played around but were careful not to go too far. Sex was there, don't get me wrong. I just wanted to finish high school first before having children. Along with teenage life came teenage problems. I would drink beer with friends. We also smoked weed and thought we were cool by being able to keep it from those who we felt shouldn't know. I hid it as long as I could and that wasn't very long. One summer night I came home tired and high. I walked into the house and went to the dining room to place my keys on the table as usual. I did not notice that I had dropped a bag of weed on the floor by the table. Then I took my high and tired behind upstairs to my room and fell into bed.

High School

Early the next morning, I heard Stephanie downstairs yelling at someone. I could not make out what she was saying, but I knew it was serious. I went downstairs to find her and Tom standing by the table in the dining room. I asked what was going on.

She opened her hand and said, "I found this on the floor this morning and you two were the last to come in the house last night."

It was a bag of weed, and I knew it was mine the moment I saw it. I thought, *oh shit, I'm dead.*

"Whose is it?" she asked.

Tom told the truth and said it was not mine. I lied and said it was not mine. I walked away and as I went upstairs, I thought, *Damn, I lost a whole bag of weed.*

By mid-summer, it had gotten worse. I was arrested for possession of weed, and Stephanie had to come get me out. It was not enough to keep me, but as a minor, a parent or guardian was the only way I was going home. I had time to think. While waiting in the tank, that's what it was called—I don't know if it was considered a think tank—but I had a lot of time to think while handcuffed and nowhere to go. I thought long and hard. I felt small; I felt low and when I thought of my sister coming to get me; I thought, *This is the end. She is going to kill me and kill me dead.* I thought, *If I was not handcuffed to this bar under the bench in this holding tank, I would kill myself.* But I had to wait until my sister got there and she would kill me. That was torture. That was a criminal injustice.

When Stephanie and Tom arrived, she never got out of the car. Tom came in and said she was mad and was waiting in the car. I cried and, with a trembling voice, told him she was going to kill me. I told him I had never been in any trouble and now I was a dead man. I told him she would not want to hear what I had to say. What could I have said? I dried my eyes and wiped my face as we walked to the car. Once inside the car, I was surprised my sister did not say a word. She just cried. My heart broke into a thousand pieces as the tears fell from my eyes. I could have never imagined how hurt she was knowing her baby brother was arrested for possession of marijuana. It was hard to see my sister cry like that and to know I was the cause. I sat in the back seat, quiet and alone. It wasn't until we had walked in the front door and were standing in the living room that she spoke.

"You are not to leave this house for thirty days. You have to do all your chores, no television and no phone calls, nothing at all."

I had my freedom taken away as I was sentenced to stay in the house for thirty days. I could not handle that. I could not handle hurting myself and hurting her. So, without thinking, I said, "You might as well expect me not to live here anymore."

"That's fine with me."

I left home and found out really soon that I had nowhere to go. I walked the streets, played basketball with friends, and slept in the park for a few days. I even tried to stay up all night, but with nothing to do, that did not work. Finally, I called my sister, Margaret, and told her the whole story as if she did not know by now. I asked if I could come live with her for a while, and she said yes. She told me she was my mother, and she would always be there for me. She reminded me that school was the most important thing in my life right now and that was all I needed to be thinking about.

I had to put that behind me, and I did because school became the dream to achieve for this Black kid who was now running wild. Margaret set it up for me to go to the school of my choice in West Philly. Although I did not live there, she had a friend to say that I was living with her and that allowed me to get into University City High School.

I had set my sights on this school in West Philadelphia. It was a fairly new school, and I thought it would be good to leave the neighborhood, even if it was just to go to school. I had heard about the school from a friend who lived around the corner near 5th Street. We called him by his nickname: "Hop." His brother was named after a president: "WW." Hop was attending University City, and he told me all about the school and how to get in. I never forgot him for that reason.

University City High School sat on the corner of 36th and Market Street. It was the big elephant on the block. University City High was different. Of course, it was the first time I realized that a school could have more Black students than any other group of people. The staff were mostly Black, the teachers were Black, and the hall monitors were Black. It was a great feeling and a wonderful sight. I tried to fit in and the only way I did that was because I was Black. I still dressed preppy, although I did not wear a tie. I carried a briefcase, but it was soft leather with zippers and a flap to cover the main section where the books went. I noticed that most students just carried books and others wouldn't dare do that. It was high school; it was Black, it was freedom, and I loved it.

I had enrolled in one of the top programs. I had a choice of the motivation program or the magnet program. I only chose the motivation program because the class started at 8:00 a.m. and ended at 2:30 p.m. This was the same schedule for Catholic school, so I took it. The first quarter of school was a major adjustment for me. I could not understand how much freedom the students had. They ran the school. They came to class when they wanted. Some never went to class. They got high in the restroom, played music in the lunchroom, and were rude to the teachers and staff. It was the students' world, and they ran it. Not very well, I must say.

Being new, I spent most of my time by myself. I read the map of the school floor plan to locate classes and sat in the back to see everything in the room. By the end of the first quarter, I was sitting in the back of my homeroom class and a student was reading the class roll sheet. When he asked, in a loud voice, "Who is Steven Matthews in ten-zero-one? This is ten-0-one. Steven is on the honor roll." He turned and looked at the teacher, who was pointing in my direction. He then turned and said, "You are on the honor roll, and you don't say anything to anyone? I will show you around and introduce you to everybody. They need to know that this homeroom class has a student who is on the honor roll." Ron P. was cool. He got good grades and dressed well. He knew a lot of students. Every time he saw me in a class or passing in the hall, he would introduce me to someone and boast of me being on the honor roll.

I felt better about meeting people but remained a little to myself because I had to continue to get the grades to prove I could do it. Living with Margaret was okay. We did not live in a nice house like Stephanie and her kids, but it was home. Margaret was proud of me. I went to school every day and came straight home, did my homework, and went to bed. I said little. I really had little to say. School was everything. She would tell me how proud she was of me and that she had all the confidence in the world in me going to college. She reminded me of that more times than I could remember.

During my eleventh-grade year, Margaret had to move to South Philadelphia. It was one of the worst sections in the entire city. It was the deepest part of South Philly where the projects were the low end. I hated it. I hated everything it stood for. I hated the way it looked: vacant buildings, trash everywhere, and the people were always looking to make something happen, something bad, that is. The projects were a wasteland, and it made the lives of poor people that lived there a waste. They had nowhere to go and nothing to do with a lot of time to do it. It was depressing to even enter that section of the city. Many times, you would not get many visitors if any. They would be too afraid of something bad happening to them. No one came to visit at night. When it got dark, it was a bad idea to be outside when you lived in the projects. The projects made the ghetto. If you lived outside the projects, it was a wonderful place to live. When you lived in the projects, you had a better appreciation of the ghetto because anywhere other than the projects was better. The projects conformed the lives and minds of the people who lived there. It made people angry at the situation. People who directed their anger toward everyone else, and violence became second nature for many. For, some it was the first. The projects were where the least of the least and the worst of the worst lived.

The situation at home got worse. My sister was no longer able to provide for me. I was in high school and needed things. Money was tight, if there was any money at all. I tried working in a fast-food restaurant, but coming home late at night was a scary thing. The problem was working affected my grades, and that was not good at all. By mid-year, I quit the job and did some research. I had to find a better way while still in school. A social worker instructed me to visit the social security building for information that may assist me and my dilemma. I spoke to a representative. She was tall, thin, blond hair, blue eyes, and very nice. She had a picture of Muhammad Ali on her desk with the phrase: "I am the greatest."

I asked her, "Are you the greatest?"

She laughed and said, "I am at what I do."

I smiled in return I told her I was still in high school, that my mother had died when I was a baby, that my father was not at home and because of his age, was getting social security. I asked if there was a possibility that I might be entitled to some kind of benefits. She told me in order for her to do anything, I must get my birth certificate, mother's death certificate, and my father's social security number. She said when I returned with that information, then she may be able to help.

Two weeks later, I returned with all she had asked for and I gave it to her in a yellow folder. She told me to have a set and she would return shortly. When she came back, she asked if I had any other brothers or sisters around my age. I told her I had a brother named Mark, who was five years older than me. She told me I may be eligible for benefits and some back benefits because when my father began receiving his benefits, he stated he did not have any young children. She said for me to return in one week and she should have more information for me and to bring my brother's social security number with me.

The following week after school, I was in her office and nervous to know more about the situation. She told me she has good news that I was to receive back benefits for at least eight years or more. She said to wait, and she will return with some papers and my first check. When she returned, she had a check for a little over 3,500 dollars and said this is to hold me until all calculations are in and the rest will be sent in the mail. When she handed me the check, I said, you are the greatest. I signed the forms and went straight to a bank in downtown near Broad and Market Street. The Bank was called the Providence National Bank. I opened the account with 3,000 dollars. The money came right on time. I felt like a new man. Honestly, I felt like I was a rich man. I took only what was over the $3,000 home and gave it to Margaret. She wanted more, but I told her I needed it for school, and she understood. She never put anything before my education. Now I could get many of the things I needed for my last two years in school.

I had the second check sent to my sister, Cynthia's, address. I would not dare have it sent to the address of the projects. It was a little over 5,900 dollars. It is funny how things change when money is a factor. Cynthia was reluctant to give me the check once it came. We had a long talk, and she decided to give it to me because she realized I had nothing to complete school with and no one to help me. I made the bank deposit for 5,000 dollars and took the rest home. I gave some money to my sister Margaret, but it was not enough. She wanted more. We got through it, and I began to plan for my graduation, which would be the following year. The feeling was one I could never explain. I had a little money, my grades were honors, and no one could tell me what to do. I purchased a 69 Chevy Camaro from an auction. I brought clothes I badly needed and some of the pleasures as well. I bought a nice stereo and color television.

Just when everything seemed to be going so well, wasn't so great at home. Margaret and I were not on good terms.

We barely spoke and when we did, it was in disagreement. I think this was too much for her to handle, but it was too much for both of us to adjust too. Margaret told me I had grown up too fast. She said I was selfish and cared for no one other than myself. I told her that she may be right, but I will be gone soon, and I will need to figure out things on my own. I called my sister Stephanie and told her the situation as if she did not already know. It was amazing to me when something happened, the whole family knew it before I told them. It was not my intention to hurt Margaret. I was growing in a way no one seemed to understand. I was truly becoming a man, making some adult decisions for myself. There was no male figure in my life to teach me, guide me, or direct me. I was alone in that area with no one to talk to. I moved in with my sister Stephanie and her family for the second time. Little did I know this would be the last time I would ever live with my sister Margaret. I will never live with her again. This goodbye was really goodbye to the woman I always called mom.

CHAPTER 3

Graduation

I moved in and it was another adjustment to make. I had the rules of the house, and her kids were her kids. I was just her baby brother living there to complete my twelfth-grade year in high school. It was okay. I still had a lot of freedom with which I had to be responsible. I continued to dress fashionably and dated older women or girls who carried themselves as women. I remained on the honor roll in school, which gave me a new sense of maturity. Women did not act like girls. They had their own cars or an apartment or both. They had no curfew. This was very important to me because I could stay out late on weekends. I did not have to explain to their parents why we were out past 11:00 p.m. on a Friday night. This got me in a different kind of trouble. My sister, Stephanie, complained about me seeing a woman her age. I told her we go out, eat, and have fun together. I had to reaffirm that there was no sex going on with these older women. The one problem I didn't have to worry about with these women was they took care of themselves. I did not have to worry about them getting pregnant, which was something that was very common with the young girls in the neighborhood. I remember when my best friend, Bert, got his girlfriend pregnant. It was as though his whole life was over. Every time I saw him, he was worried about being a father.

Once, my sister came into the house while I was on the phone and yelled in my face, "You better not come home with any babies!"

I looked up at her in great confusion and said, "I'm not."

When she walked away, I thought to myself, *She must be going through that female change of life called menopause.* Another time she jammed me up and asked, "How come you don't talk to any of the girls on this block?"

"Because they are just girls. I like women."

She left me alone after that. I could not think of talking to my sister about sex. Plus, most of the girls on the block came up pregnant. Nina, Janine, Sookie, and Pam were pregnant around the same time, just to name a few, and there were others. I was not getting caught up in that mess. So, I lied and said I was not having sex. My sister had to have known that some woman was rolling in the sack with her baby brother.

Graduation came fast. There were the taking of pictures, picking out class rings, and continuing to make the grades to ensure I would walk across the stage. Before that was prom night. I rented a nice car, a dark brown Monte Carlo. It matched the suit I wore. It was beige. I paid for her gown and all the extras. I took a grade-school sweetheart who did not attend my high school. Her father did not want her to go because I was Black and she was Puerto Rican. She went anyway, and I was happy . We had a wonderful time as young adults. We went to the after-prom party but did not stay. We got a room for the night and comforted each other because we knew this would be our last time together.

Only one family member came to graduation, and that was Stephanie. Her husband came later because he had to work that day. After graduation, we went to Stephanie's house, where the other family members showed up. Many of them I had not seen for years, and it would be years before I would see them again. It was time to enjoy the moments with family.

The School District of Philadelphia

Board of Education

has

Public Schools through grade 12

UNIV. CITY HIGH

June 19 1979

School

FORM H 92—CERTIFICATE OF GRADE COMPLETED—SCHOOL DIST. OF PHILA. (OCT. 1970)   Principal

---

UNIVERSITY CITY HIGH SCHOOL   YEAR ENDING JUNE 1979

REPORT OF

PUPIL NO.   CURR. MOT   GRADE 12   GROUP NO. 111

ADVISER MR DIRADDO   PRINCIPAL DR DAVIS B MARTIN

EXPLANATION OF RATINGS

SUBJECT

Achievement in relation to work planned for the subject, including use of time and materials, neatness and care in work, preparation for and participation in class work. Ratings from beginning of year to date.

BEHAVIOR

Obedience to regulations, respect for property and rights of others, honesty, truthfulness, courtesy, effort.

SUBJECT RATING SCALE

A — Excellent
B — Good
C — Average (Fair) — Lowest Certification mark for college
D — Clearly below average (Barely passing)

P — Passing
E — Failing · Subject may have to be repeated
F — Failing — Pupil may be prohibited from repeating subject.

BEHAVIOR RATING SCALE

1 — Excellent
2 — Satisfactory
3 — Unsatisfactory

Parent-Teacher Conference Date

SIGNATURE OF PARENT OR GUARDIAN

Your signature above indicates that you have examined the report, it does not necessarily signify your approval.

Please Read the Other Side of This Report Carefully

THE SCHOOL DISTRICT OF PHILADELPHIA
PUPILS REPORT, SENIOR HIGH SCHOOLS AND
AREA VOCATIONAL · TECHNICAL HIGH SCHOOLS   Form S619C-REV. 1/76

ATTENDANCE INCLUDES

SUBJECT	PERIODS PER WEEK	FIRST REPORT GRADE	FIRST REPORT BEHAVIOR	SECOND REPORT GRADE	SECOND REPORT BEHAVIOR	TH'RD REPORT GRADE	TH'RD REPORT BEHAVIOR	END OF YEAR GRADE	END OF YEAR BEHAVIOR
ENGLISH 4	05	B	1	B	1	B	1	B	1
TITLE 1 R	05	A	1	A	2	A	1	A	1
SPANISH3P	05	B	2	B	2	B	2	B	2
SH COL BD	05	B	2	B	1	A	2	A	1
URB PLAN	05	C	1	B	1	C	1	B	2
PE 3-4	04	A	1	A	1	A	1	A	1
HEALTHED3	01	A	1	A	1	A	1	A	1

UCHS GRADUATED

	FIRST	SECOND	TH'RD	END OF YEAR
Adviser's Rating of Pupil's Behavior-as a Citizen in Homeroom, School and Community.	1	1	1	1
GRADE NEXT YEAR — DAYS PRESENT	33	74	121	172
DAYS ABSENT	1	2	33	6
TIMES LATE		0	0	0

Bloomsburg State College

My brothers, Lewis, Eric, Ray, and Mark, were all there. I had not seen them in I don't know how long, and it was not as though we lived far away. We all lived in the same city. My sisters, Cynthia, Margaret, and Debbie, came and gave me kisses and words of encouragement. They were proud of me. Little did I realize, and to my knowledge, that I was the only family member to have finished high school or that I was the second one to have done so. Who was the first? I don't know. It was a wonderful occasion to have my immediate family in the same house after so many years apart.

It seemed to have come so quick, and it was over just as quick. Stephanie asked, "What plans do you have now that you have graduated?" This was a routine of hers. She would ask, "Are you going to find a job or go to college?" I was waiting for a college to send an acceptance letter, which was due in the summer for the fall semester. I at least wanted the summer off to give me a break. The Air Force sounded good to me, but I had heard that if you did not have perfect vision, you could not pilot a plane. That idea was shot down because I wear glasses. She could not wait. When she heard a recruiter was coming to visit from a small college up north, Stephanie welcomed her with open arms.

Two weeks later, I was on my way to Bloomsburg State College for their summer program. I was talked into it and rushed off, thinking I would be there only for the summer if I did not like it. I did not understand the rush to get me out of the house. How could I have missed it? I wasn't her son. I was just her brother, and it was time for me to go. I was out of high school for two weeks. That thought ran through my head for days. Now I was in a strange town that held less than two hundred Blacks in the whole town. I had just gotten out of high school, and I was back in school, a school where most of the faces were white. I hated it and wanted out badly. I hated being there, but had no one to come get me and nowhere else to go.

I buried the feelings, and I hid them well. One day in my dorm room, I sat alone thinking and drinking. I did not know who to trust. I felt empty being away from the world as I knew it. Once again, I was alone, truly alone. It was then I realized I was on my own. The thought of leaving my family felt good, but what was this feeling in the pit of my stomach? The feeling of loss. What was this worth to come so far and to have to leave it all behind? It was this feeling that made me realize for the first time in my life that I loved my family. I cried. It was overwhelming, and the pain was astronomical. The tears fell like rivers. My stomach was in a knot. My fist clinched as I lay in the fetal position in the middle of the room. I had to take care of myself and there was no one to assist in that department. There were no counselors to help a poor Black kid become a man. There were no books to teach that subject. Only life could teach it and to learn it, I had to keep living. The days went by and so did the weeks. I did okay for that summer, well enough that I returned that fall.

College life was harder than high school and the problems were much harder to solve. My grades were not so great and for the most part I was failing. But that did not seem to matter what mattered was I was not where I wanted to be. It took much longer to study and more time to learn the subject and no matter how much I put into it I failed just the same. I began to realize I was not as smart as I thought or there were forces working against me making me fail in class. After a while it no longer meant much to me, so I began to party more. Drinking, smoking and partying have a way of allowing one to forget what is wrong for a moment. You don't have to care about anything just the party. While getting high there are no feelings of loneliness, no worries of despair, no thoughts and no cares. The partying started on Wednesday and ended on Sunday. Classes were scheduled in between.

I called home many times to talk to my sister about what was going on but most of the time I cried on the phone. She would say things to cheer me up, but she never said I could come home. I did make some new friends but all of them got high in some form or another I guess that's why we were friends. I thought I had fallen in love once when I met Dori. She was a very attractive sister who really seemed to care for me. What we had between us only last for the time we were in school. I managed to keep many of the things I did away from her not wanting to hurt her in any way. By mid-year I was snorting cocaine and taking speed pills. This was a new high and it felt good. I had tried acid but did not like the trip. So, I stayed with what I thought I could handle not knowing that it was really handling me. At times all I wanted to do was get high. I lived for the weekend because I knew I would get high from Friday to Sunday and that was considered a good weekend.

I had a connection that supplied me with a pound or two of weed and I began to sell to keep a dollar in my pocket. But mainly I did it to keep some pot around for my habit and close friends. You cannot live off of nickels and dimes especially when you had a habit of your own to manage. By now the Social Security had run out a long time ago but the monthly check of one hundred and four dollars continued as long as I was in school. I sold weed to make the extra money but there was never an extra dollar. I sent the check home to my sister to save for me. I knew it would not last long, so I asked her to put it away until I came home. I had a close call with the campus police that could have ended my life as I knew it as a college student.

One day after class I had went to my dorm room and on the way I saw the campus police walking around and looking around my dorm building. So, I quickly ran to my room and looked out the window and saw many of the police officers at the rear of the building I realized something was up and I had to act fast. I took the weed out of my closet it was at least a pound or more put in a dark plastic bag and went in the hall. I knocked on the door next to my dorm room and when he answered I asked to come in. I told him I needed a favor, and I needed it right now. I told him to hold this for a little while but don't smoke any of it until I come back. I told him that if he did this for me I would give him anything he wanted. He agreed. I went back into my room and waited. Within ten minutes or less there came a knock on the door not just any kind of knock a police knock. They tend to knock on doors with a flashlight or a night stick the stuff they use to knock on heads with.

I opened the door, pretending like I was reading a book or studying. In the hallway, two police officers were already present. Shortly after, two more forcefully entered, while another one stood in the doorway, holding the door open.

I tried to be calm and asked, "What is the problem?"

One officer said, "We will ask the questions."

I was shaking in my pants and thinking, *I hope my roommate did not hide any weed on my side of the room as he often did.*

They searched the room, looking under the beds, through the closets, and in the dresser drawer at personal things. They took notice of all the empty alcohol bottles that decorated the room.

One officer said in a deep voice, "Drink a lot?"

STANLEY MASSEY

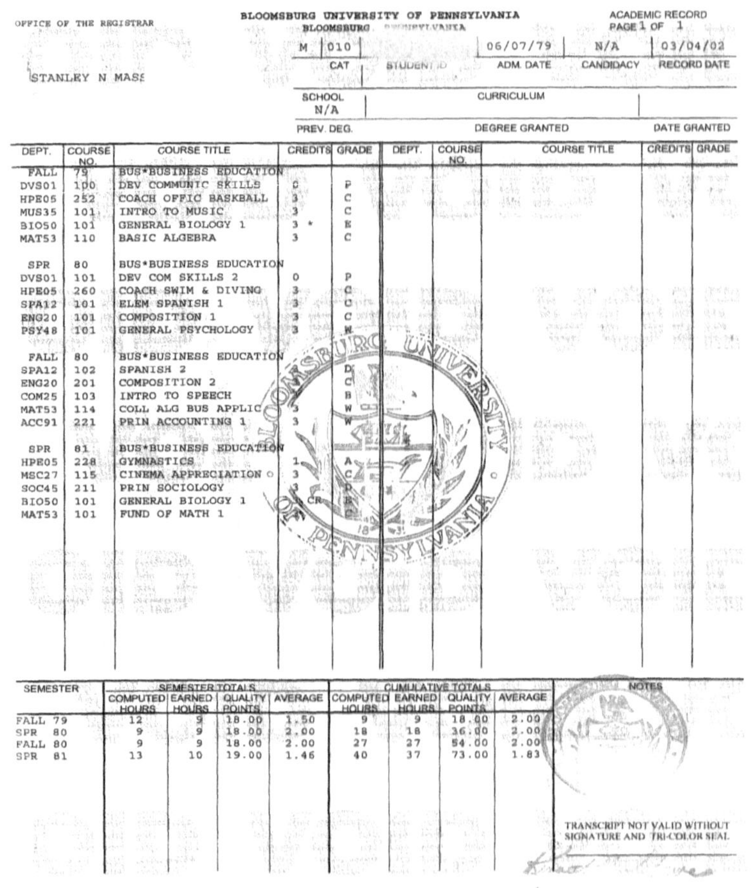

M	010		06/07/79	N/A	03/04/02
	CAT	STUDENT ID	ADM. DATE	CANDIDACY	RECORD DATE

SCHOOL N/A	CURRICULUM	
PREV. DEG.	DEGREE GRANTED	DATE GRANTED

DEPT.	COURSE NO.	COURSE TITLE	CREDITS	GRADE	DEPT.	COURSE NO.	COURSE TITLE	CREDITS	GRADE
FALL	79	BUS*BUSINESS EDUCATION							
DVS01	100	DEV COMMUNIC SKILLS	0	P					
HPE05	252	COACH OFFIC BASKBALL	3	C					
MUS35	101	INTRO TO MUSIC	3	C					
BIO50	101	GENERAL BIOLOGY 1	3 *	E					
MAT53	110	BASIC ALGEBRA	3	C					
SPR	80	BUS*BUSINESS EDUCATION							
DVS01	101	DEV COM SKILLS 2	0	P					
HPE05	260	COACH SWIM & DIVING	3	C					
SPA12	101	ELEM SPANISH 1	3	C					
ENG20	101	COMPOSITION 1	3	C					
PSY48	101	GENERAL PSYCHOLOGY	3	W					
FALL	80	BUS*BUSINESS EDUCATION							
SPA12	102	SPANISH 2		D					
ENG20	201	COMPOSITION 2		C					
COM25	103	INTRO TO SPEECH		B					
MAT53	114	COLL ALG BUS APPLIC	3	W					
ACC91	221	PRIN ACCOUNTING 1	3	W					
SPR	81	BUS*BUSINESS EDUCATION							
HPE05	228	GYMNASTICS	1	A					
MSC27	115	CINEMA APPRECIATION	3	C					
SOC45	211	PRIN SOCIOLOGY	3	D					
BIO50	101	GENERAL BIOLOGY 1	CR	B					
MAT53	101	FUND OF MATH 1		E					

SEMESTER	SEMESTER TOTALS				CUMULATIVE TOTALS				NOTES
	COMPUTED HOURS	EARNED HOURS	QUALITY POINTS	AVERAGE	COMPUTED HOURS	EARNED HOURS	QUALITY POINTS	AVERAGE	
FALL 79	12	9	18.00	1.50	9	9	18.00	2.00	
SPR 80	9	9	18.00	2.00	18	18	36.00	2.00	
FALL 80	9	9	18.00	2.00	27	27	54.00	2.00	
SPR 81	13	10	19.00	1.46	40	37	73.00	1.83	

I replied, "It's legal."

Another officer, while searching my closet, found my weed pipe. "What have we here?"

I said, "I don't think you came here looking for that."

After about twenty minutes of making my room look like a disaster had hit it, they left.

I closed the door and waited a while. I looked out the window to make sure they were gone. I said a quick, "Thank you, Lord," and went next door.

Kevin was cool. He said, "Is everything all right? They will not be coming back."

I said, "They have been made a fool of once today. I need to get rid of this in a hurry." Before leaving, I gave Kevin an ounce of weed and asked, "Is that enough?"

"Man, this is more than enough." We shook hands, and I was on my way.

I called two other friends and told them about the situation and they agreed to help me get rid of it quickly. Of course, we did not throw it away or flush it down the toilet. That would have been stupid. Besides, there was money to be made, and that's how I made it.

On the next school break, I went home to visit family and friends. While there, I had borrowed my brother, Ray's, car. It was a beautiful Buick Rivera, turquoise with white leather seats. I had with me three hundred speed pills that I brought from school for twenty-five dollars. I knew on the streets I could get a dollar or two for each pill. I had a sandwich bag filled with marijuana and a couple of rolled-up joints for my personal use. I was on my way to make a few dollars while driving through South Philadelphia. I noticed in the rearview mirror a black and white cop car with two white cops following me. They followed for about two blocks before flashing the lights, pulling me over. I had time to put the stash under the seat, but the joints were still in my pocket. They both got out the car and walked up to the driver's side of my car.

One officer said, "The reason we pulled you over is you ran the stop sign."

I knew damn well I did not run a stop sign, but I didn't argue. I was thinking, *Give me the ticket and let me go.*

They asked for my driver's license and told me to get out the car.

"What do you do?" one officer asked.

"I go to school up north."

One officer searched the car and found the pills and weed that were under the seat. "Look what we have here."

The other officer said, "Is this how you get ahead in school?"

They were not looking for any answers. I was young, Black in a nice car with drugs in it and that's all they needed.

Scared and trembling, the sudden urge to piss came over me. I held it and said, "No, that's not mine."

They put the handcuffs on me anyway and put me in the back of the patrol car. My heart was pounding, my thoughts were confusing. I could not think of my own phone number. The only thought that came to my head was, *Your ass is going to jail.*

We pulled up at the police station as they took me through the long process of humiliation—the feeling of being less than human was evident. I was only given orders to which I could not respond. I was told to do this and do that. Stand here and turn this way. There was the constant sound of chains, sliding bar cage doors locking, and the jingling of keys at all times. When it was quiet, I still heard these things in my mind because I became a prisoner in my own head. The feeling of being on the inside was much worse than words could ever explain. The moment I was in the cell behind bars and that cage door slammed behind me, I knew and realized I was less than nothing in a cell. I was in a place where I did not want to be.

I was locked up in a cell, alone and scared. My mind told me I was there because of the system. I blamed it on the people who ran the system, and they ran the world. The truth of the matter was that I was locked in that cell because of my own stupidity—nothing more and nothing less. Freedom as I once knew it was no more.

I was in early enough to see the judge the same day. He set a court date and released me to my brother, who came to pick me up.

Once outside the jailhouse, Ray asked, "Where is the car?" I told him it should be where I parked it because I don't remember them having it towed. My brother told me we have to go get the car because he had some man-made drugs hidden in the door panel of the car. The car was in the same spot where I had parked it, but my brother said he would drive it home. The court date was set for thirty days, and the wait was enough to drive me crazy. I knew to continue to do well in school as this would or may help in my defense.

At eight o'clock in the morning, I was sitting in the courtroom waiting for my name to be called. Nervous does not explain my condition on that day. I must have gone to the bathroom at least ten times. I did not know a person could piss that much, but I did. I was not much of a praying man, but on this day, I had one prayer. "Please, God, don't let me go to jail." Finally, my name was called, and I rose to hear what he was saying.

The judge ran off with the reasons why I was in court on that day. He told me what I was charged with: possession of an uncontrolled substance with the intent to sell. I was charged with possession of marijuana with the intent to sell. Then he asked me, "What do you have to say about the charges?"

I said, "None of that belonged to me. The pills were not mine. The marijuana was not mine. All I had on me was the couple of joints that were found in my pocket. I was driving a borrowed car." I told him I was home on vacation from school, and I didn't have any criminal record of any kind. I told him the officers pulled me over and said I ran a stop sign but never gave me a ticket for that violation. I told the judge that while I was facing one officer, the other officer searched the car, and I did not see where he found that stuff."

The judge took a second to think and then he said, "I am going to dismiss this case because of insufficient evidence." To hear those words was music to my ears. Then he said, "But if I ever see you in my courtroom again for any reason, I will lock you up."

I smiled and walked out. Once on the court room stairs and I saw the blue sky, I looked at the sky and said, "Thank you, Lord. You answered my prayer."

Ace Deuce Trey

I returned to school with a new outlook on life and the freedom I had. I would put my head in the books and try to do better. This thought lasted only for a short time because my friends were still there doing the same thing. I never talked about what happened because I did not trust many people. We partied more than we studied; we drank, smoked, and did drugs. We were young and were having a good time. Called home and talking to Stephanie. I told her that soon I would come home for the summer. She suggested I start sending some money home so I would have something when

I got there. I agreed and sent money home every month. In my mind, she would save it for me so I could have some spending cash for the summer. But my sister had another plan for me and the money.

When summer came, I was excited to be going home. I said my goodbyes and had finished all my packing. My brother, Eric, came to pick me up and drive me home. He helped pack the car, and we were on our way. As brothers, we never said much. He would ask a question and I would give a short reply. The few hours of driving went fast, and we were at Stephanie's house before I knew it.

When we pulled up in front of the house on Parrish Street, he said, "Don't take anything out of the car. Just go and tell Stephanie we are here."

Excited to be home, I ran into the house and called for my sister. She answered from the kitchen. I gave her a hug and said, "We are here, and I need to get the stuff out of the car."

"You don't have to take anything out of the car. I have a surprise for you."

"Why I don't have to take any of my things out of the car?"

That's when she dropped the bomb on me. Stephanie looked me in the face and said, "You don't live here anymore." She picked up her purse and said, "We are going to take you to where you live now."

I said nothing while following her to the car. What could I have said? What was there to think? I couldn't think of one word.

Once in the car, she said to Eric, "Let's go."

Still, I said nothing, and it was apparent they had this all planned out. I sat in the back seat, thinking about how the family was so damn good at keeping secrets. I was hurt, but I could not show it and there was nothing I could do but sit there.

We pulled up in front of an apartment building on the corner of Fifth and Girard. Stephanie opened the door of the apartment and said, "This is where you live now. You are grown, and this is your apartment." It was empty, just as empty as what I was feeling in my heart.

I asked, "Where is the furniture?"

She said, "You have to buy it." She handed me the keys as my brother was already unloading the car.

The three of us stood in silence in the middle of the room for a moment. I looked at the two of them with piercing eyes and a closed mouth. Finally, I hugged them and said, "Goodbye."

As they left the apartment, I closed the door behind them, and I closed the door to my heart one more time. I stood in the room with my things from college and thought for a moment. The family I once knew was not the same today. The home as I knew it to be was not mine anymore. I thought, *Here I am alone again.*

The apartment was small. It was called an ace deuce tray because it had one room on the first floor, which was the kitchen, with two rooms on the second floor—a bedroom and the bathroom—and a third room on the third floor.

I took my things to the second floor and, with what I had to work with, made the room as livable as possible. I had my thirteen-inch color television, a stereo, and my clothes. When I was finished, the room looked like my dorm room, but it was mine. I sat down to make a list of the things I needed, and the thought came to me: why make a list? You need everything. So, I figured to get things as I needed them while living in this tiny apartment. The one thing that rang in my head was I was grown and able to do as grown people did. I could stay out or come in as I pleased. I could have girlfriends stay as long as they wanted. Yes, this was what I enjoyed about being grown. To me, it was freedom.

The summer went quickly. I had done what it took to survive on my own. I had money every month to pay rent, buy food, and the things to sustain a young single man. But now it was time to think of what the next step will be. I had to decide whether to return to school or work to maintain the apartment and the life of a bachelor. In the final few weeks of summer, I decided I wanted to extend my summer and take a trip to California. Although I was considered grown, I still discussed my plans with Stephanie. I told her I would go to California for two weeks and would return to school afterward. She had a few questions, and I could see the doubt on her face, but she could not tell me what to do.

She only said, "If that is what you want to do, then it's fine with me."

I planned my trip to California, deciding I may not come back at all, so why plan to do so? I sold all that I could sell of the things in the apartment and what I could not sell, I gave it away. I would use the money for necessities once in California. I made a flight reservation for one-way from Philadelphia to Los Angeles LAX. I kept things simple and said little to anyone about my true intentions. I did not want it to be a big fuss over what I had decided.

Finally, I made sure that the apartment was empty, just like it was when I moved in. I had my two bags packed and my plane ticket in my pocket. I took a deep sigh of relief before closing the door behind me, thinking I may never return to live here again. I went to the street where Stephanie and Cynthia lived to say my last farewell. Since Cynthia's house came first, I stopped there first. Cynthia and I talked for a while, hugged and kissed each other for the last time. She wished me well and told me to go see Stephanie before leaving. I began the walk to Stephanie's house with only one thing on my mind: I was finally leaving this city. When I got to the door, I rang the bell and immediately the door opened. Cynthia must have called and told her I was on my way. Before I could say anything, she began walking toward the kitchen.

So, with her back to me, I said, "I am ready to leave. My flight takes off in a few hours."

Without answering, she went into the kitchen. I stood in the living room for a moment, not knowing what to do next. I called her name softly as I began walking toward the kitchen. She was looking out the small window next to the built-in oven. I called her name again. "Stephanie." I moved toward her. She turned around, and I saw the tears rolling down her face. We hugged ever so tightly and cried together.

She said, "You are not coming back." Those words pierced my heart as the water filled my eyes and ran like rivers down my cheeks.

I kissed her wet cheek and said, "I'm sorry." I was sorry for so many reasons. More importantly, I was sorry for all the pain I caused.

I walked away and picked up my bags at the door without looking back. I had a friend take me to the airport. Once checked in, I boarded the plane. There were no feelings of excitement or joy. It was an eight-hour flight, and I had time to think. I ordered a beer to relax and calm my stomach. I sat there staring out the small window with not one thought in mind. Moments later, as I continued to look out the window, I felt the tears roll down my face. I was crying because of the feeling in my stomach. I was leaving my family, and a piece of my soul, too.

CHAPTER 4

California

The first year in California was hard, but I had some fun during that time. I hooked up with a friend from my old college and he showed me around for a while. I slept on the sofa in his apartment. I used his car while he was at work to look for a job. In my second week, I found a job. Shortly after that, he moved out with his girlfriend to a town called Hacienda Heights. In less than six months, I had a job, and an apartment, and looking to buy a car.

I finally got a 1976 Chevy Monte Carlo, financed through a bank. Now the hunt was on. I had a job, an apartment, and a car, which I used mostly to pick up women I liked. I could go to some of the hot spots in Los Angeles and around town and pick up women. I was young and single. I called home from time to time, but the phone bill took its toll, and I could not see my money going to the phone company. Most of the time, I was bored and alone with nothing to do and no real place to go.

One afternoon while shopping, I met a nice young lady. She worked in a department store and was of great assistance to me while I was there. She was pretty, young, and very kind. I liked her and made it a point to shop in that store more often. After a few times in that store, I asked her out, and she said yes. Her name was Valerie, and she was a good Christian girl. She did not smoke, drink, curse, or got high at all. Sometimes I would think this girl was too good for me or anyone of my kind. I had good reason to think this way. I drank beer, got high, and cursed from time to time. She worked, stayed home, and went to church. This was the kind of girl I wanted.

We went out and started seeing each other more and more. As time went on, I was fed up with her situation at home, so I moved her in with me. We practically did everything together. We slept in the same apartment, in the same bed, but she would not let me touch her. She said she was saving herself for marriage. It was hard, but I knew eventually it would happen. We were like kids. We played and went to amusement parks. We were happy, and it showed. It only lasted a year. One year without touching the girl I spent most of my time with got dull. I did what I did before I would go out and leave her alone. By the time we started playing with sex, the sparks were no longer there. I thought she had someone else, and she knew I was not out always alone. It wasn't long before she had become pregnant. She knew it was mine. I didn't want any kids at that time, so I thought, *Momma's baby, papa's maybe.* I had every excuse not to have the baby, but nothing worked. She went to stay with her father for a few weeks. I worked, had girls over, stayed out late, drank, and got high, but nothing filled the void like Valerie.

When Valerie returned, it was time to get serious. We found a small two-bedroom house with a shared front yard. Shortly after moving in, Valerie went into labor. It was a difficult process, but she pulled through and I became the father of a beautiful little baby girl we named Marie. Marie was named after my oldest sister, Margaret Marie. I had promised Margaret that I would name my daughter after her because she had raised me as her son when our mother passed away. I was filled with happiness to become a father; having something that belonged to me brought me a sense of pride. A year later, Steven Jr. was born, and I thought this should be all the kids we needed. I was happy and excited, but inside my spirit, I was full of fear.

Shortly after his birth, I noticed the fear became more suppressed and I medicated by drinking more. I was between jobs, could not keep up with bills, and used beer as my way to not think. On one occasion, I remember going out to celebrate the birth of my son with a few friends. I got drunk and tried to drive home, but a few blocks from the house, I hit a parked car. The impact caused me to hit the steering wheel face-first. My bottom lip was severely injured, almost completely cut off by my lower row of teeth, leaving it barely attached by a small amount of skin. When the police arrived, my car had to be towed, and I was taken to the hospital. One doctor, when he saw my lip, said it would be easier to cut the lip off and go from there. I said no with the best mumbling I had. A second doctor, much younger than the first, came into the room to look at my hanging lip. He asked me to uncover it and he promised not to touch it. After examining it for about two minutes, he said he could save my lip.

A nurse gave me something for the pain, but I felt all the twenty-seven stitches he had put in my lip to hold it together. The doctor told me the swelling may go elsewhere because it was so badly swollen when he stitched it up. The swelling went to my face, and it swelled to the size of a basketball. His instructions were to keep ice on my lip, morning, noon, and night. I had to carry ice everywhere I went to keep my lips on ice. The ice helped the swelling and reduced the pain immensely. It took two months to heal completely with minimum scarring.

It became more and more difficult to keep up with paying the bills and doing what I wanted to do. I fell behind and we had to move to another location. We found a small one-bedroom apartment and tried to make it work. During this time, I was chauffeuring and working as a sales representative for the same company. I made plans to marry Valerie in a small chapel. We could not afford much, so it would be the kids and some of her family. On that day, her sister had my kids, and she did not bring them to the chapel to be a part of the ceremony.

It was important to me to have my children as a part of something so very precious between their mother and father. The problems escalated. Valerie's uncle came to me, asking to borrow money. He said he would pay me back double. I lent him two hundred dollars, and he promised to double it. I went with him, and he scored cocaine, and this was when I was introduced to rock cocaine. I had not tried it before and did not know that it only took one hit to be hooked. He mixed it, cooked it, and rocked it, then asked if I wanted a hit. I tried it and the rest was history. I was hooked. I wanted more. When it was all done, he said I had smoked up my money. It wasn't long after that she left me, took the kids, and moved in with her mother. I found myself walking the streets, sleeping out in the cold, and begging for food. I had lost everything—the family, the apartment, the car, the job— it was all gone, and I was all alone. Many things were going through your mind. The one constant thought was: How in the hell did I get into this mess? When you think of a way out, you think of death, which is a way out of the mess, and it is a way out of life. The only problem with that thought is which way is the quickest and least painful? But I really wasn't ready for that yet.

I remember one night while walking the streets, a dog behind a gate barked and scared my spirit out of my body. It scared me so badly that my body froze in that spot because I could not run. But my inner being had zipped across the street. I saw my spirit on the other side of the street, and I saw my body stuck in this walking position. I had to tell my spirit to come back to my body so I could move. In those few seconds, I experienced an out-of-body experience. I was a nervous wreck after that. I thought, *Damn dog*.

Days became weeks and weeks became months and I was totally confused. One afternoon I found myself walking the streets, and it hit me. One of my sisters had told me if I ever needed her to call. There was one problem. I couldn't remember her phone number. My mind was so full of drugs that it was hard to think let alone think of a phone number that I hadn't called in over ten years. Finally, I called the operator and asked to place a collect call to my sister, Cynthia. I thought for sure the line would be busy due to all the kids that lived in the house. Someone would be on the phone tying up the line. But as miracles do happen, my sister answered the phone and accepted the charges. I told her all I could in the time I had on the phone. I told her I was on drugs. I told her I had lost everything. I had lost the family, the job, the car, the apartment, and I had been living in the streets for some time now. As I told my sister of all my failures, the tears fell, and I knew she was crying on the other end of the line. When I was finished she said in a trembling voice, "Can you get to the airport?"

"I don't have any money."

"Start walking and by the time you get to the airport, a plane ticket will be there for you to bring you home." She made me promise I would go straight to the airport. I promised.

It took me two and a half hours to get to the airport. Once there, I walked up to a departure counter and told the lady my name; she asked for identification. Once I had shown her my driver's license, she said, "We have a nonrefundable flight, one-way to Philadelphia, scheduled for takeoff in one hour." She gave me instructions on how to get to the boarding gate and handed me a ticket. I went into the first men's room I saw to wash my face and rinse out my mouth that tasted like an army had marched through it barefoot. I tried to fix myself up but there was no fixing me up. I was a mess, and I knew it. I boarded the plane, found my seat by the window, and was ready for something to eat. I hadn't eaten a good meal in months, so whatever was on the menu, I wanted it, and I knew it would be the best meal I would have in a long time. I don't remember what it was, but I remember it was so good it put me to sleep for most of the eight-hour flight.

My brother, Ray, met me at the airport. We greeted each other with hugs and were on our way. We talked but not much; I thought my sister would have told him everything, but she didn't. The sisters were good at keeping secrets in the family. I should have remembered that. Thirty-five minutes later, we were at Cynthia's house, and I was in for a surprise. The entire family was there, some I knew, some I had forgotten, and the rest I wasn't sure if they were family or friends of the family. I think my brother must have known something was going on because he let me go through the door first. The family greeted me with lots of hugs and kisses. The tears fell and for several minutes continued to flow. To them, it was a happy moment to have a member of the family return after being away for so many years. For me, it was a sweet, bitter moment. It was sweet to be in the presence of loved ones after so long. Yet it was bitter knowing the mess my life was in. But at the time, that did not seem to matter to the family. I was home, and that was reason enough to be happy.

I settled in with my brother, Eric, and his family. He had a house on Wyoming Street with an empty bedroom. He said his two sons could sleep in one room. He and Gale, their mother, would sleep in another room while I could have the third bedroom. I found a job as a representative in a secondary college and did very well on the job. I made a salary plus commission. My position was to get potential students enrolled in the school's education programs. I enjoyed the work and could pay Eric for allowing me to live with him. A few months later, my wife and kids came to stay with me at my brother's house. During this time, my brother,

Mark, was in the hospital. Stephanie was worried because she had not seen him for a while, so she asked Ray to check on him. When Ray got to Mark's house, there was no answer. Ray forced the door open and found Mark unconscious on the floor.

I went to see Mark in the hospital. He was in a coma, hooked up to machines and wires to monitor his breathing and his heartbeat, and IVs administering fluids and medications. His hospital room was like something you would see on television, but this was real. To enter his room, I had to wear a mask and a gown and cover my shoes with the hospital shoe covers. I stared at my brother with the deepest of heartfelt sorrow. He was only five years older than me and the years of drug abuse made his face appear much older. He was motionless and barely breathing. The picture came to memory of that day as a kid when I found Mark passed out on the kitchen floor and the dope needle still in him. I said a short prayer over him, asking God to have mercy on him with the family. I put my face against his face and felt the roughness of the wrinkles. I whispered in his ear that I loved him and that he had a lot to live for. I told him we were what Mommy left to the family. I mentioned he hadn't seen his beautiful niece and nephew, my two kids, yet. I felt the tears roll down my face, and I saw tears roll down his cheek. I stood up and stared out the window as I prayed again.

Stephanie entered the hospital room. "Hey, Steve. I didn't know you were here."

I told her I got off work a little early today.

She told me to take a good look at Mark. "This could be you if you don't stop doing drugs."

To Stephanie, drugs were drugs. My brother shot up heroin. I never did. I smoked rock cocaine, but to her, it was all the same. At least the end results were the same. I left the hospital in a fog, not knowing what to think or what to do. What was I to do? My brother was near death and I was dying on the inside. I continued to work, but after work I got high. I became quiet with less and less to say. My wife and I decided it was time to move out of my brother's house and get something of our own. This kept me busy and on the right track for a while. I found a house on the west side of town. It was an older house with four bedrooms upstairs and lots of fine wood in all the rooms downstairs. My wife and I decided on the house, and we met the seller, and I made the down payment. With the closing payment, it was due at the same time I had to pay my brother for living with him. My brother refused to wait for his money and the seller refused to wait any longer as well. My wife and I were heartbroken, but did not want to hurt my brother. I paid Eric for the time we lived there. My wife and I decided it would be best not to get the house but to move back to California instead.

I thought it would be nice to take the train back. Besides, it was too expensive to fly with the entire family. We did not want to wait too long trying to save the money for the plane

NORM *Dayen*

7244 RISING SUN AVENUE
PHILADELPHIA, PA. 19111

REAL ESTATE - INSURANCE
NOTARY PUBLIC

(215) 342-4500

CUT OFF DATE: 10-24-88

PROPERTY ADDRESS: 1420 LINDLEY AVE
PHILA, PA.

MINIMUM PRICE	$ 32,000.	OFFER ABOVE MINIMUM	$
MAXIMUM MORTGAGE	$ 31,200.	MORTGAGE UNDER MAXIMUM	$
DOWN PAYMENT	$ 800.	DOWN PAYMENT	$

CLOSING COSTS

1% Funding Fee	312
Taxes	700
W&S Adjust.	
Trans. Tax.	
Interest	138
Insurance	240
Rec. deed-Mtge	

TOTAL CLOSING COSTS $ 1,390.

TOTAL CLOSING COSTS $

Total funds needed to buy $ 2,190.

Total funds needed to buy $

DEPOSIT NOW $ 800.   BALANCE AT TIME OF SETTLEMENT $ 1,390.

****

Monthly payments for $ 353.66 Mortgage at 10% Interest for 30 Years

Principal & Interest	$	275.33.
Real Estate Taxes	$	58.33
Insurance	$	20.00
	$	353.66 TOTAL

(OFFERS ABOVE MINIMUM PRICE MUST BE 3% OR HIGHER THEN THE LIST PRICE)

(INVESTORS REQUIRE 10% DOWN PAYMENT)

Veterans Administration

PROPERTY MANAGEMENT NO
PM 398394

SALES LISTING—LOAN GUARANTY DIVISION

1. LISTING DATE: 10/14/88 — [X] ORIGINAL [ ] REVISED

2. ADDRESS OF PROPERTY (Include ZIP Code)
1420 Lindley Avenue
Philadelphia, PA 19141

3. TERMS PRICE: $ 32,000*
4. CASH PRICE: $ 28,800
5. LOAN BALANCE PAYABLE IN: 30 YEARS
6. DOWNPAYMENT: $ 800
7. INTEREST RATE: 10

8. DESCRIPTION OF PROPERTY

TYPE OF CONSTRUCTION			FLOOR FINISH	ROOFING DESCRIPTION			CAR GARAGE	STORM SASHES
Brick		DETACHED			6	NUMBER ROOMS	CAR GARAGE	STORM SASHES
	X	SEMI-DETACHED			3	BEDROOMS	CAR PORT	STORM DOORS
		ROW	Pine	Built up	1	BATHS	BUILT-IN	GUTTERS
NO. OF LIVING UNITS 1	2	STORIES	WALL FINISH	TYPE HEATING AND FUEL	1	KITCHENS	ATTACHED	REFRIGERATOR
		SPLIT LEVEL		Gas	1	LIVING ROOM	DETACHED	DISHWASHER
SQUARE FEET 2274	100	% BASEMENT	Paper	Steam	1	DINING ROOM	FIREPLACE	GARBAGE DISP.
			BATH FINISH	CEN. AIR COND.		FAMILY ROOM	X ENCL. PORCH	WASHER
APPROXIMATE LOT SIZE		CRAWL SPACE	Tile			REC. ROOM	PATIO	DRYER
21 X 141		SLAB		APPROX. AGE OF MAIN BUILDING 75 Years		UTILITY ROOM	FENCE	OVEN & RANGE
		FINISHED ATTIC				RM.		[ ] BUILT-IN

9. TYPE OF STREET SURFACE: Asphalt
10. STREET ACCESSORIES: [X] CURB [X] SIDEWALK [X] STORM SEWERS [X] LIGHTS
11. APPROXIMATE ANNUAL TAXES: $ 700.00
12. ZONING CLASSIFICATION: N/A

13. UTILITIES | PUBLIC | COMM. | INDIV.

	PUBLIC	COMM.	INDIV.
WATER	X		
GAS	X		
ELECTRIC	X		
SANIT. SEWER	X		

14. BALANCE OF SPECIAL IMPROVEMENT ASSESSMENT: $ N/A
15. ASSESSMENTS TO BE PAID BY: [ ] VA N/A [ ] PURCHASER
16. SALES COMMISSION RATE: 6

17. DATE OF ABSOLUTE TITLE IN VA: Pending [ ] ACTUAL [ ] ESTIMATED
18. NAME OF TENANT:
19. UNIT:
20. MONTHLY RENTAL: $
21. UTILITIES INCLUDED IN RENT:

22. REMARKS

INSTALLMENT CONTRACT *Or any reasonable offer will be considered. "THE BUYER IS TO BE MADE AWARE THAT THE PROPERTY MAY CONTAIN LEAD BASE PAINT." No repairs by VA. The VA makes no warranties or guaranties of any nature whatsoever. Purchasers should make a physical inspection of the property prior to settlement. Buyers must obtain their own use Registration Certificate if required. Buyer may apply for funds to make repairs that are considered necessary to make the property safe, sound and sanitary. Maximum additional loan amount is $3,000.00. Applicable Loan Guaranty Bulletin is #36-88.

fare. For the next few days, I did not talk much. I went to work. After work, I got high. My wife had gotten pregnant with our third child, and we wanted to get into a house of our own to raise the children. When those plans fell apart, I only wanted to leave Philadelphia once again. We talked about what went wrong, and how we should not have told anyone what our plans were for the house. Other family members said that they thought my brother was jealous, and that's why he didn't want to wait for his payment. It was all water under the bridge now. I was leaving this forsaken city, and I was taking my family with me.

Inwardly, I knew I was the problem. I was not good for my family, brothers and sisters, wife and kids. I was not good for anyone, not even for myself. So, we packed up, said our goodbyes, and boarded the train for a three-day trip across the country to California. We had no set plans, and with no place to go or live. We only knew we were leaving Philadelphia, putting behind us another part of our lives that didn't work out. The trip was not bad. We got to see the country through the view car. We talked, ate, spent time with the kids, and got plenty of sleep. When we arrived in Los Angeles' Union Train Station, my wife called her younger sister to come get us. She was reluctant to do so, but came, anyway. We arrived at her parents' house on Eighty-Fourth Street within an hour. There were no big hellos or warm welcomes. It barely came in. Minutes after our arrival on Eighty-Fourth Street, it was apparent that I was not wanted there. My wife and I talked. She told me that her family said that she and the kids could stay, but I had to leave. I realized that this place was only for her, and the kids and I were not a part of this family anymore. I hugged and kissed my kids goodbye, not knowing where to go with little money in my pocket.

Once again, I was out in the streets and all that had any meaning to me was somewhere I was not wanted. I was sad, lonely, and filled with grief. The tears fell as I walked the streets, but they were meaningless. In my heart, I said I would get back on my feet and I would not look to depend on them ever again. I was bitter, angry, upset, and cast down. I was weak, confused, and torn from within. I hated those people. I had done many things for them and when I needed help from them, there was none. My thoughts were, *I will show them, and I will make it so I will not have to ask them for anything again.* I was in the streets again, full of pain, with nothing and nothing to lose. So, it was all I could do was get high, and I did. I went to an old friend and asked if I could stay with him and his family. He said it would be okay, but I would have to sleep on the floor. I agreed. Where else would I sleep? I found another job and started visiting my wife and kids. I got a small room and moved my family in with me. Shortly after that, Valerie had our third child. It was a boy, and we had agreed on the name Sam. It felt good to have another son. I was so very proud. I thought there couldn't be no more children. We couldn't afford to have any more children.

It wasn't very long before I messed up again. While Valerie was home with the kids, I would go out and get high. We only could pay rent weekly. We actually lived in one of those motel places where you could pay weekly. Truthfully, I could not afford an apartment or a house because I could never save enough for a deposit or down payment. It got worse. I didn't pay rent one week, and the manager came and put Valerie and the kids out. When I arrived, there was a lock on the door. Management could lock you out for not paying. Because it was not an apartment and there was no rental agreement, they could lock you out with no legal action. I found my wife and kids in the nearby park. Valerie was sitting on the bench holding Sam while Marie and Steven Jr. played with each other in the play area. Marie and Steven Jr. had a unique closeness that is evident to this very day. Valerie sat there with Sam in her arms, not saying a word. There was nothing to say. I had nothing to offer her and the kids. I could not come up with any valid way to get us into another room. I had no money.

I could not imagine the hurt and pain she must have felt, to be a young mother with three beautiful loving children, one being a newborn and to have a man who was nothing she thought he would ever be, a loser in every sense of the word and less. After a few minutes, she spoke in a low, soft voice.

"The kids and I will have to go back and stay with my mother. You will have to find a place for yourself." She did not lift her head, not wanting me to see the hurt in her eyes. But I knew she was right. I also knew I had broken her heart once more. Again and again, I could not figure out why I continued to mess up the lives of the people I loved, as well as my own. The things I said I would never do, I did. I said I would never get on drugs. I was. I said I would always be there for my family. I wasn't. I saw Valerie saddened, hurt, and brokenhearted because of me. Because I could not be a father, a husband, or a man to those who loved me, I felt less than human. It was happening all over again. My family and I had to separate one more time. We said our goodbyes with tears in our eyes.

For a moment, I sat alone on the park bench, remembering the time before Sam was born. Marie and Steven Jr. were three and two years old. I was doing well on my job as a limousine driver. We had a good life. Marie and Steven were in preschool and doing okay in an all-day school. It was time to show her I loved her, and I did honestly love her. I married her for many reasons, but the one that was the most important was she was the mother of my children and that was the best reason. They were all I had, and I never wanted them to leave. My worst fears were taking place as they walked away in the distance. What happened? In such a short time, I saw my life go from fluffy to flat. I mean very flat. I could not bring myself to say I love her and the kids because everything I did was contrary to that.

I wish I could say that time went by fast, but it didn't. I was out of their lives for two and a half years. I would call, but most of the phone calls were tears of sadness and despair.

I saw them on weekends and that time was limited. When visiting, it was obvious to Marie and Steven Jr. that their father was sad. They had a way of seeing in my heart and soul. They also loved me there as well. I stayed away and worked hard to get on my feet. I stayed from place to place and sometimes no place at all. Valerie found a small one-bedroom house for her and the kids. I knew there was no room for me, and I did not ask. It was her own place, and she could do as she pleased. She would allow her family and friends to visit, but I had to wait for her to bring the kids to me. When I went to the house, I had to get the kids and be back shortly.

I slowed down in using and drinking while Valerie took off in the fast lane of her life. She had a house she was renting, a car, and other men. She had it all. I was a thing of the past. I haunted her memory with a life of bad times. There was a sour taste in her mouth. She hated me and now she could put me out of her life altogether. I could do nothing to her or for her. I could only support the kids. Valerie was now the free woman she always wanted to be. She was free of the burden of having me around to destroy her beautiful life. The life I took advantage of and turned it into the mess it was for so many years. She needed no one but had everyone. She was happy again. She had everything and what she didn't want, she pushed it away, particularly me. It was obvious she didn't need or want me. Think about it, I had lost everything. I was selfish and not good for anything or anyone. I couldn't even do it for myself.

The pain continued to grow, and it grew even more. When I visited, I saw the men in her life. Her phone rang all the time. Whenever we were alone, which wasn't too often, we were interrupted by the phone. She would go to another room to talk to him. She treated me rudely and showed me I didn't matter anymore. She had no regard for what I said or felt she was no longer there for me.

For the next two years, I took my family through pure hell. I took things in exchange for drugs. I took my wife's wedding ring and got high with it. I figured she was no longer a wife to me, so she didn't deserve this ring. It was only an excuse to go out and get high. But when I was finished, reality hit hard. I had nowhere to go, and I was out in the cold again. Somehow I bounced back, continued to work and got an apartment in a small town called Azusa, but I was never really happy there. I had a girlfriend who would come and stay, but I only wanted to be with Valerie. So, the relationship didn't last. I had a dispute with two other users, and one was a gang member. The police got involved and there was a court decision. I will say that it did not go in their favor.

I moved to Pasadena, and it was there I cleaned up my life again. I kept my job and called the family more often.

I also visited as much as possible. Valerie would bring the kids to visit me from time to time. I would take them to the park, and we would walk through city hall. We would walk through the mall and see a movie. But when the kids were asleep, I would drink and get high. Valerie caught on to this and took the kids and told me it would be a long time before I would see them again. I later moved into a larger apartment in the same building. I worked hard at trying not to use drugs. I bought new clothes, shoes, and a queen-size bed, but the things did not satisfy me. I was not complete. There had to be more. I was getting high again.

This time, I became a loner. I had no real friends. Relationships with other women were out of the question. None of them pleased me. I was not willing to allow another woman to take the place of Valerie. I also did not want to give them what I would only give her. It was hard to trust. I did not trust anyone. I did not want to open my heart to anyone because I knew it would only be closed, eventually. Relationships, I let them go. So, I made my kids my friends and only them would I trust. I tried to visit on weekends, but Valerie had the upper hand on when I could see the kids. She was the power force in their lives. She controlled what went on between me and the kids. So, I called every day. I called before work. I called during work. I called after work. I called at night. I called and called. My phone bill would be a hundred dollars and the only number would be that of my kids.

Valerie and I talked some. She would let me visit and on good nights, she would let me sleep over. I would go to work from there and return. If I got high, she would send me home to my lonely apartment. It was not all great or peaches and cream. There were many times when I knew her other man would call, and she would go into the bedroom to talk to him. Many times, when I would arrive at the house, she would have to leave out. She would tell me she had something to do. She would stay out all night and come home the next day. I guess she had to give him his because she wasn't giving it to me. We slipped away again. She no longer wanted to talk to me. She would not hear anything I had to say. Talking to her was like talking to a wall. There was no communication, none at all. She was colder than ice toward me. I went to my apartment to clear my head. My daughter would be eight years old in August and I wanted to be a part of that. I had a little time to prepare, so I did. Valerie had planned to give Marie a birthday party in the park. Valerie had invited her family and friends. Marie wanted it to be special and wanted me to be there. I brought her a new bike and rode the bus from Pasadena to South Gate with her gift. I arrived early and had her gift and a gift for my sons as well. The kids and I greeted each other with smiles, hugs, and kisses. It was really great to see them again. I gave them a few dollars to top things off. I had to look good for the special occasion, so I even wore a new T-shirt with shorts and tennis shoes. It was Marie's eighth birthday, and I felt good about that. I spoke to their mother and glanced toward her family and lover. There were no words for them. I was there for my kids.

Lovers

The kids and I talked for a while, and I tried to look as if I was having a good time. It felt really strange being a part of something, but realizing your part doesn't matter. I told the kids to enjoy themselves while I took a walk around the park. They would not have it, so they walked with me. We walked, talked, and laughed as we used to do. By the time we returned to the event, the rest of the guests had arrived.

Valerie had set the stage for the perfect birthday party. The tables were beautifully decorated with matching ribbons hanging from nearby trees. The food and refreshments were well placed on the tables. Valerie's mother, two sisters, and a few of her girlfriends with their men were sitting around the tables talking and laughing. It looked like the family I once knew. As we approached, I told the kids to greet their grandmother and family. I would not keep them from the people they loved, and I wanted them to know that. I watched from a distance, not wanting to get too close and not wanting to offend anyone. I nodded to their grandmother as a jester of respect when our eyes met. It was at this point I realized what it meant when it was said you can be in a party with many people and yet be alone.

As the party progressed, the activities became more playful. The water guns and water balloons were now present, and people were running around avoiding getting wet. Jack, Valerie's lover, began chasing her with a water gun and a water-filled balloon. Another person joined in the chase and when Valerie turned to run in another direction, she ran into the arms of her lover. He picked her up and spun her around. It was the kind of shit you would see lovers do in movies or read in story books. It was priceless. They silenced the guests, and all eyes were fixed on them. My heart stopped for a brief moment while my eyes filled with tears. I turned to walk away, but my kids were in hot pursuit.

I felt their tiny hands in mine as they tugged and asked, "Where are you going?"

I kneeled down and said it was time for me to leave. They knew the reason and did not ask. They were connected to their dad and loving in that special kind of way.

Steven Jr. said, "But you are our dad and that's not right." He was sharp and knew he could say what was on his mind and in his heart.

I told them, "Your mother is grown, and this is what she wants. I am no longer a part of that, but remember, I will always be your dad.

Marie told me she liked her new bike and how much she really loved me. She always tells me I'm the best dad.

Steven Jr. asked, "Do I have to wait for my birthday for a bike?" Then he went on to say, "No other man will ever be my dad."

I said, "No, I will bring you yours next week." Tears roll down his cheeks as I talked. I wiped his face and said, "You have to be strong, and it will be all right."

Sam, while crying, said, "Why don't you just stay?" He said he wanted to come with me.

"Now is not a good time," I told them, "And daddy must get his life together first, then we will be together."

It was difficult to tell what we were all feeling at that moment, but it was a lot of hurt, pain, separation, and loss all in one. We all embraced, crying and loving together. They loved their dad. I knew it and I did indeed feel it. As I stood and walked away, tears rolled down my face, heartbroken. My thoughts were my world, the world I knew was crumbling apart little by little. I saw it fading away through teary eyes.

The following week, I brought Steven Jr. his bike and gave gifts to Marie and Sam. I spent time with the kids, and it was a great time. It was a time to just enjoy the day. I kept money in my pocket and that was because I also stayed clean. I would not get high for weeks at a time. I rented cars to pick up the kids on the weekends so we could drive where we wanted to go. I also came in my work car, which was a limousine, to take them for a joy ride.

Valerie allowed me to stay at the house from time to time. But I knew to always keep my apartment. I knew when she got angry or tired of me, she could and would send me home. Valerie did whatever she wanted to do. I had to follow her rules. She was in charge. She was the boss. She had the power that could inflict pain, and she did it as a way to keep in control. But as usual, I was the blame, and it was my fault. I was not there for her. I was not her husband. I was not a father to her kids. I was another cokehead, and she had no problem letting me know it. She would call me a crackhead or a basehead. To her, there was nothing worse.

Today was Friday, and I had been straight all week. I had cashed my check, and the money would go to the family. I gave Valerie money for the bills and food. Some went into her pocket for personal expenses. There was a portion for the kids as an allowance. The remainder which was just a few dollars, went to me. We ate dinner, and it was very enjoyable. We were all there together, talking and eating as we used to do. I had a beer with dinner and felt fine. We cleaned up and watched a movie when it was apparent that the kids needed to go to bed. We kissed them good night. Shortly after that, I felt the urge to go to the store for more beer. I realize now it is the line many men have told their women with no intention of doing what they set out to do. I told her, "I'll be right back." She tried to stop me, said it's not important, said please don't go. I went anyway. I was gone the entire night. Later, I found myself riding around on my son's new bike with nowhere to go and trying to get a clear head.

Finally, I went back to the dope house. The Latino guy respected me for some reason. He treated me differently than I saw him treat others who came to him for dope. I was looking for more dope and I knew I could get it from him, but I had no money. I asked him to hold my son's bike until I could get some money to pay him for what he would give me. At first, he said no and said for me to go home with the bike. I think he just did not want to be a part of a kid losing his bike because his dad had a drug problem and the respect he had for me. Finally, he gave in and took the bike as a trade for about twenty or fifty dollars' worth of rock cocaine. I told him I would be back in a couple of days with the money. He said okay. The bike was all I had of value, and it wasn't mine. The coke was all I wanted.

I went to a dark secluded place and made a pipe out of aluminum foil to smoke the rock. I put a large piece of coke in the pipe, lit the lighter, took a huge toke on the pipe, and inhaled. It was then I realized what I had done. I had sold my son, Steven Junior's, bike for dope. The magnitude of that thought spun my mind and turned my stomach. I was high, spinning, and sick all at the same time. I was at an all-time low. This was something I thought I would never do. I cried like I've never cried before. This was from my soul. This cry was from the deepest pit of my stomach, which was now in a knot. I cried out and said, "Lord, he is my son and I need your help."

I threw everything away, the pipe, the dope, and the damn lighter. I threw it as far as I could throw. I walked back to the house with streams of tears flowing from my eyes. Valerie was reluctant to let me back in. I told her what I had done, and I told her I not only needed help but wanted it as well. I woke my kids up and told them what I had done. I told Steven Jr. that his dad sold his bike for dope.

With tears in his eyes, "He said it's all right, Dad," and hugged me.

I told my daughter, Marie, that her father had a drug problem. I told my son, Sam, that I needed help and I had to get it before it was too late. With tears, hugs, and kisses, they gave me their love and support and told me it would be all right. The kids and I cried, while Valerie just looked on hurt but tearless. I told Valerie to call her brother, who had completed a drug rehabilitation program a year ago. He came over right away and told me about the program. He prepared me for what was to come and what was expected. A few days later, I entered the Palace Program for Drug and Alcohol Rehabilitation.

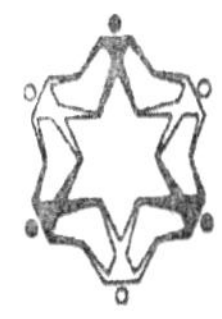

**People Coordinated Services
of southern california, inc.**

CASTLE COMMUNITY RECOVERY CENTER — EAST
4771 S. Main Street / Los Angeles, California 90037
(213) 233-3342

Evelyn D. Knight
Executive Director
PEOPLE COORDINATED SERVICES

Virgie P. Walker
Program Director
PCS CASTLE SUBSTANCE ABUSE

PROGRAM SITES

CASTLE ADMINISTRATION ☐
1221 South Western Avenue
Los Angeles, California 90006
(213) 735-1231

CASTLE DRUG PREVENTION ☐
& EDUCATION PROGRAM
1221 South Western Avenue
Los Angeles, California 90006
(213) 735-1231

CASTLE EARLY INTERVENTION ☐
3021 South Vermont Avenue
Los Angeles, California 90007
(213) 732-9124

CASTLE RESIDENTIAL ALCOHOL ☐
ABUSE PROGRAM - WEST
1319 South Manhattan Place
Los Angeles, California 90019
(213) 734-1143

CASTLE RESIDENTIAL DRUG ☐
ABUSE PROGRAM - WEST
1319 S. Manhattan Place
Los Angeles, California 90019
(213) 734-1143

CASTLE OUTPATIENT ALCOHOL ☐
ABUSE PROGRAM
3021 South Vermont Avenue
Los Angeles, California 90007
(213) 732-9124

CASTLE OUTPATIENT DRUG ☐
ABUSE PROGRAM
3021 South Vermont Avenue
Los Angeles, California 90007
(213) 732-9124

CASTLE EAST - ☐
COMMUNITY RECOVERY CENTER
4771 So. Main Street
Los Angeles, California 90037
(213) 233-3342

CASTLE SUBSTANCE FREE ☐
LIVING CENTER
2211 South Hobart St.
Los Angeles, California 90018
(213) 737-9109

1-19-94

P.M. Group
100 W. Clarendon
Suite 2000
Phoenix, Arizona 85013

Stanley Massey entered the Castle program on 7/26/93. This client has been in the Castle East program for six months. The rent for the Castle East program is $300.00 a month. Mr. Massey received DIB for 90 days while in the Castle program. Client has paid $1,149 in Rent. Client owe as of this date 700.00 for Rent. If you have any questions feel free to call me.

Thank you
Operations Specialist
Lula Dison

CHAPTER 5

The Palace

The Palace or House, as it is called, is a two-story building with a basement, bedrooms, and counseling rooms for addicts who are fortunate enough to get into the program. Located in the heart of Los Angeles in the forty-seven-hundred block of Main Street, one would not know it was there by looking from the outside. It assists those who have the desire and the will to get off or stop using drugs, alcohol, or both. The program is not a picnic or a walk in the park. It is a process.

I entered the program during the third week of July 1993. During this time, I was writing and had not gotten high for at least a week. Someone asked me, "What brought you to recovery?" so I wrote it down and followed the process. I could sum up what led me to recovery with just one word: drugs. To elaborate further, it would be drugs and alcohol. But primarily, I brought myself here to get myself together. I needed my whole being restored again so I could function in the real world in the real way the world functions. I brought myself here to find out who I was and to know where I was going.

Recovery for me is the search for self-worth. I needed to know how valuable I was, not just to others, but to myself. It was necessary to know what this value meant. I had hoped that understanding this great value would give me the knowledge that I was also great, or at least great in my own special way.

Today, I think about being alive, being a better person, and being blessed. I attain more information as time goes on and things are revealed to me. Recovery is the means to the end of alcohol and drug abuse. It is the finding of a person inside the person. Recovery may be the tarring down of the old and constructing or reconstruction of the person I was meant to be. Recovery is the desire to change and the ability to adapt to or with the change. So, what brought me to recovery? I wanted to change.

The Palace was a twelve-step program, and I had to take part in each step as an addict in order to understand my addiction and why I had this problem. Some steps would be quite obvious to the non-user, but to the addict, they were far beyond sight and comprehension. With Step One, I had to admit I was powerless over alcohol and drugs and my life had become unmanageable. It was so very true. I did not have an ounce of power over the drugs or alcohol and my life was way out of my control. The lack of control over the substance happened when I was not doing anything productive. I wanted to get high. The only thing productive was work. But I did not seem to produce much. Work kept me from doing what I really wanted to do, and that was getting high. So that was the sign that I could not control the urge to get high. You figure this out by understanding that you get high for any reason. It's hot outside, you get high. You had a good or bad day at work, so you get high. There is a party, and you get high at the party. Life is not going well, so you get high. This is also called self-medicating. For whatever reason, you get high or medicate and that is the powerlessness. I also realized the unmanageable part of my life. How could I manage anything when my whole life revolved around getting high?

With the help of the Palace Program and others like me, I could achieve the power and strength to put an end to what was causing me a slow death. This program is the foundation I need to build upon so that I may never have to return to the deadly effects of the mind-altering drugs and chemical substances. I have not been in the program for very long and I had learned some very interesting things. I've learned alcohol is a drug because it falls under the same definition as drugs: any chemical substance that causes a change in the structure and/or function in living organisms. Alcohol causes a change in the brain and the body, which are both living organisms. I have also learned that there are only three places for me as long as I continue to drink alcohol and do drugs: jails, institutions, or death. I had been locked up because of my drug abuse and being in that institution, the only thing left was death. Learning this showed me I only had one of the three left and death didn't look too promising.

With this in mind, I proceeded to Step Two. I had to believe that only a power greater than myself could restore me to sanity. Was I insane? Let us look at insanity for a minute. Insanity is doing the same thing repeatedly, expecting different results. I kept getting high, thinking my life would get better. Here is an example of my insanity. Let's say I was walking down a street and up ahead I saw a sign that read: THERE IS A BIG HOLE IN THE MIDDLE OF THE STREET. I walked up to the hole and fell in after reading the sign. The next day, I walked down the same street and saw the same sign and the same big hole. Again, I fell in. On the third day, I did the same thing and got the same results. I ultimately fell into the hole. Now that was insanity. It was only when I changed and went in a different direction or down a different street that I could expect different results.

The power greater than myself I call God. You can call it whatever you want. I believe God is the power that gave me another opportunity to make decisions that will affect my life positively rather than negatively. I can make decisions that cause change in my life, and I can adapt to the change. Understanding I have a higher power I call God, I now have to turn my life and will over to Him. This is the Step Three. Remember, I made a mess of my life doing it on my own. So, if I can't do it, I give God to it. If He can't do it, then it can't be done. This is my understanding of that higher power. He can do it all.

The days became weeks in the Palace, and I was okay and doing well. It was structured, and I didn't have a problem with following the rules and regulations. There were a lot of rules in this program and there was a rule for everything. If you got into any trouble, they would ask whether you knew the rule or if you adhered to it. Knowing and following the rules was connected to being successful in this program. Being a co-ed facility, the rules were more intense. There was to be no contact whatsoever with females, and vice versa. You had better not get caught looking at a female too long because it could cause you to break your program and fail in the recovery process. You had to always keep in mind that you came to the Palace to recover from alcohol and drug abuse, not to meet the love of your life.

This leads me to Step Four, which states I had to make a searching and fearless moral inventory of myself. When trying to apply this step, I realized there wasn't much to inventory. To be fearless and moral, I lost those qualities a long time ago because of my addiction. I had to redevelop fearlessness with a sense of morality while accumulating an inventory of myself. The question was asked, "How far would you be willing to extend yourself?" To find this thing called sobriety, I had to be prepared to go to great lengths for an extended period.

Then a counselor told me, "It isn't about the distance or the time it will take to achieve sobriety; rather, it is about the level of desire. You never know how far, far is until you go it."

I asked, "How long is long?"

He said, "Not long."

It might take a lifetime, but I was willing.

Step Five was the admitting process. I had to admit to God, myself, and another person the exact nature of my wrongdoings. There were so many people I had wronged; I could not think of them all. So, I admitted I had wronged God. I wronged people who cared about me and those who didn't care. I wronged myself by destroying my mind and body with alcohol and drugs. The nature of my wrongs was pure selfishness. I thought I was not hurting anyone while I was getting high, and that thought was selfish and wrong. There was one brother who showed a genuine concern for me in the Palace. I had asked questions about the AA Book and was puzzled because it seemed so basic and simple up to this point. He went to his room and returned with another book for me to read. It was the *Twelve Steps and the Twelve Traditions*. He told me to read the two books together and at a much slower pace. He said, "With that desire, you will find it."

I was now having visitation by my wife and kids, and I had returned to my old job as a driver. When we were together, the kids and I hugged and kissed, but Valerie just said, "Hello." I understood, so I didn't ask for more. I was happy to see and be with my children for the couple of hours I had.

The kids always asked, "When will you be coming home?"

My answer was, "It will not be too long."

Valerie usually asked, "How are you doing?"

I would say, "Fine."

My job allowed me to continue to contribute to the family, and I knew that was the main reason for Valerie's visit. I also gave something to the Palace and put a little aside for personal things. My counselor told me she should come to some meetings to learn more about the recovery process. He dropped hints of her having her freedom and for me not to get my hopes up too high, thinking of returning to the family I once had. He was really a great counselor, and he gave it to me straight—with tough love. I listened because I believed he knew what he was talking about.

Step Six told me to allow God to remove all my defects of character. I realized I had a lot of defects, but there was one I knew I needed to remove: the attitude that I was not like everyone else. I would say, "They are messed up. I am not all that bad. At least not to me." So together with Step

Seven, I humbly asked Him to remove that attitude and all of my shortcomings and my defects of character, whatever they might be.

The Rash

I made a list of all the people I hurt and attempted to make amends to them. This was Step Eight, and it was a little difficult to do. My list was of all loved ones or family. To make amends to them was not too hard, but to make amends to some of those ex-friends was a different story. You see, many of my associates still got high, so for me to achieve sobriety and maintain it, I had to disassociate myself from them and that environment. I made direct amends to everyone I could and made it a point not to hurt or harm them intentionally. I actually told them I was sorry, and I did not use any excuse. It was heartfelt and my heart said to all those people, "I am truly sorry." This was me moving through Steps Nine and Ten: taking a personal inventory of myself and promptly admitting when I am wrong. Sometimes I was wrong and may not know it, therefore when it was brought to my attention, I could add it to this step and apologize for it as well.

Step Eleven moved me in an entirely upward direction. I sought through prayer and meditation to improve my conscious and spiritual connection with God as I understood

Him, praying for knowledge of His will and the power to carry it out. Each night when I thought all were asleep, I would get on my knees and pray. I would pray to be healed and restored as He would have me to be. I would ask and pray for wisdom, knowledge, and a better understanding of Him and what He expected of my life. I prayed for the strength to stay away from cocaine and alcohol and being able to do this, I believed He would continue to bless me. Step Twelve was for me to practice all these principles in all my affairs.

In the Palace, I saw many things. Some residents told sad stories that brought tears to my eyes. I saw residents leave on good and bad terms, some of those you heard about later who did not make it. Through it all, I prayed and continued to pray. It opened my eyes to learning how to deal with life on life's terms. Life happens. How you deal with it is up to you. Life was happening for me at the Palace and while I was a part of it, I had to practice what I was being taught.

I caught a rash that started on my back. It had spread to my arms, legs, neck, and chest, and now it was on my face. The Palace had sent me to a couple of clinics, but each one did not know what it was, and whatever they gave me to treat it did not work. The rash had gotten so bad that I itched and scratched all the time. It got worse than that. Where skin touched skin, the rash ate away at the skin. Behind my knees and elbows and under my arms, raw flesh itched and burned. After visiting a few clinics that could not help, I went to

Martin Luther King (MLK) Hospital. A white male doctor came in to see me, but he left and came back with another white male doctor. They looked at me and asked questions. I could see two things about these doctors. One, they were afraid to touch me, and two, they didn't have a clue of what this rash was. They talked for a minute among themselves and then said, "We will send another doctor in to see you."

A few minutes later, in walked a young, Black female doctor who introduced herself as a skin specialist. She asked, "Do you mind taking off all your clothes?" Without answering, I did so, and she examined my entire body. She asked a few questions as I showed her where the rash had eaten away at the back of my legs, front of my elbows, and under my arms. She held my arms up and examined the rawness under my arms and on my forearm.

She used this huge medical term for the rash and told me it had the Christmas tree effect. It started on my back and spread to the other body parts. She told me to put my shorts on and she would return shortly. Upon her return, I had my shorts on and was sitting on the examining table. She handed me a few silver metal tubs of white cream and a blue and white plastic bottle of some kind of lotion. Her instructions were for me to wash all my clothes in mild liquid soup with no bleach and for me not to use bleach in my white clothes as well. She said for me to wash my clothes separately from the rest of the residents in the Palace. She said that I was to shower using

Dove soap because it was a mild soap. After showering, I was to rub the medicated cream on in the morning and before going to bed or, more frequently, to control the itching. While giving me the instructions, she was rubbing the cream on my back. It was a cool and tingling feeling. She told me it may tingle, but that was the medication in the cream, taking effect and for me to avoid scratching for any reason.

After getting dressed, I looked at her with eyes filled with water and gratitude. She must have sensed something. She hugged me and said, "You'll be okay," and to come back in a week. I followed her instructions and within that week, the rash had cleared up at least seventy-five percent of my body. When I saw the doctor that next week, she could see the results. She asked how I was doing and gave me more medicated cream and lotion, then she said, "Good luck in what you are trying to achieve." I thanked her and was on my way, feeling much better than the week before. It wasn't much longer when the rash had completely cleared up. I kept the remaining medicated cream and lotion in my drawer just to be sure.

Group

This day marked another turn of events for me at the Palace. Group was when everyone in the Palace came together in a circle to discuss their issues and, hopefully, resolve them.

The sessions could last for hours and took place at any time early morning, mid-day, or late at night. This afternoon, a counselor had something specific he wanted to teach us. He said that there were many things out there that would affect our desire to recover. The key to a successful recovery was knowing and understanding the three things that the body consisted of. The first was the pattern of thought—how we think and what causes us to think. The second was the way we feel or our emotions. The third was the action we take or how we respond in a given situation.

He then explained the behavior of addicts, saying, "First we think the thought. We think about getting high regardless of any other factor. Now, because of our thinking, we begin to _feel_ like getting high. We get the feeling, the urge or desire to get high within ourselves. Finally, we _act_ upon the thought and feeling. We take action in the direction of getting high. These are the three things that complete the person: the person being, the addict, or the alcoholic. It is this process which causes an addict to put their body in some of the worst predicaments."

The lesson went on to demonstrate how we must control what we think about. We must think of other things that are positive and productive. This thought process would give us a different feeling about things and ourselves. Then we must take the necessary action that would bring the best results. The counselor said that we must practice this every day and in time it would be a part of us. In any given situation it would be so natural to think, feel, and act more positively.

There was something to learn from all group sessions, but as addicts, we forget just as fast as we have learned. One group session took place at two-thirty in the morning. It was called because the Palace had issues that needed to be resolved. What this really meant was someone in the house got caught doing something against the rules, so the whole house was now in session. I don't recall what the problem was. All I remember is that I was awakened out of my sleep at two-thirty for a damn group session when I had to get up at five to go to work. I was so tired I could hardly keep my eyes open. But I learned something. I learned that while I was out there getting high, I could stay up all night and never get tired.

The Nature of My Disease

The nature of my disease was threefold. My addiction was a physical, mental, and spiritual disease that affected every area of my life. The physical aspect was the compulsive use of the drug and my inability to stop using once I had started. This meant that the drug was irresistible to my body and had a powerful force that would not allow me to stop, no matter how much I wanted to. The mental aspect was the obsession or the overpowering desire to use, even though I knew I was destroying my life. This was the intense abnormal idea and feeling of getting high, regardless of the effects it had. The spiritual aspect was my total self-centeredness. I was only concerned with what I wanted, and I could do whatever I wanted to do and whenever I wanted to do it. I also felt I could stop whenever I wanted, despite all the evidence to the contrary.

My disease was progressive, incurable, and fatal. It was progressive because it started out slowly and as time went on, it got worse. It progressed over the years and it was now in control of me. It was incurable because if I used I would be right back where I started. It was fatal because of the massive destruction it caused until the ultimate—death. It was cunning, baffling, and powerful. It was cunning because it was skillful and a master of trickery. It was baffling because it perplexed my mind and frustrated me in my way of thinking. It was powerful because it had absolute control over what I did.

This is the true nature of my disease. It is why I refer to it as the three threes.

1. The disease is physical, mental, and spiritual.
2. It is progressive, incurable, and fatal.
3. It is cunning, baffling, and powerful.

I now have a new profound respect and understanding of this disease. It is an abnormal condition that impairs my reasoning and functioning and has recognizable symptoms and signs.

The Palace kept us busy with something to do from the time we woke up to the time we went to bed. We had visitations, movies, drug and alcohol-free parties, outside recreation and many guest speakers. A guest speaker that made a positive mark in my recovery was Van. He was an addict who had been in the Palace and returned to give the new addicts of the house hope by telling his story and opening our minds with some things he had learned. Van was a dynamic speaker and compassionate in his way of telling about his experiences. I sat on the edge of my chair, and I took plenty of notes during his time with us. He told of how we were wrong in our thinking and sinful acts. He did not beat us down, that was not the point. He said we should recognize that the devil has power, and we should understand just how powerful the devil really is. He pointed out how we, as addicts, are conditioned by superstitions and traditions. He spoke on the number 666 being the number of the devil. He said we don't realize how this number is part of our everyday lives. Some examples he gave were one of our amusement parks is called Six Flags, the size of the American dollar is six inches in length, we have six coins in our money system: the penny, nickel, dime, quarter, fifty-cent piece and the dollar piece. Van said a woman likes a man who is six feet tall, a child starts school at six years of age, the number of pallbearers at a funeral is six, when you are buried, it is six feet under the ground.

You may be asking, "What does this have to do with recovery?" As Van explained, we are conditioned by superstitions and traditions. If the devil's number is 666, then why are so many things in our lives associated around the number 6. He asked the question, "Is this the devil's world?" He said for this and many other reasons we must remain connected to God. Van gave another example of how we, as addicts, think. He painted the picture of the man across the street. He has a house, a wife, and two kids and drives a nice car. He goes to work, plays with the kid, takes out the trash and mows the lawn. Every year he takes the family on a two-week vacation. He calls this living life.

But the addict says, "Shit, that isn't living and it sure isn't life." In his way of thinking and doing things, the addict doesn't work most of the time, avoids paying bills, runs through the alleys, eats when he can, hustles for money and gets high, sleeps during the day and walks the streets all night. He is the living dead, and says, "Now this is living." In his way of thinking and living, he is spiritually and mentally disconnected from God and must find his way back. Van said, "In closing, I came to bring you some truth and insight in recovery. Please read the book, *Alcoholics Anonymous*."

The entire room rose to their feet, chanted, shouted, cheered and clapped with joy and excitement.

Letters

I was writing regularly. I had been writing letters to the wife and kids. Valerie didn't always write back, and it was understood. I wrote to her to express how I felt and to show my concern. Since she didn't respond to the letters, I compiled them in a notebook. They were dated and kept in hopes of someday sharing them with her. In the book of letters to Valerie were newspaper cartoons that had little sayings of what love is. Here are a few of those letters. The first is titled Love.

Love

Hi Babe:

I hope this letter finds you in good spirits and full of joy. I want you to know how much I love and care for you. I think of you every day and need to say I have never loved like I love you today. I have only been here in the Palace for a few weeks, but it seems like a few years. It may have taken this to bring to my attention that you love me, by me realizing that I know that there is some love in me. All the love that is in me I want to share with only you. You are all I have ever had and all I will ever need. I am writing this with a clear head and an open heart. There is nothing that is in the way of my thinking or feelings. True, it has been a long time since I spoke to you like this. But you deserve more. I honestly hope I am able to provide all you desire and need.

I cannot say these words and not show you in some way that they are true. So, I am trying to get my mind, body and soul together so that I can at least be a whole person once again. Whole is the key because I want to be complete. Complete as a man and as your husband. This completeness is not to prove to anyone that I am trying to show my love for you. But it is a start to a new beginning. The beginning of my life without the things I used to depend on. I want to start all over again, but this time I will use what I've learned. You may ask, what exactly did I learn? I've learned that it is possible for me to love you. It is conceivable for me to say I love you. It is a true fact that there is love in the depths of my heart. It is also true that this love was revealed to me by you. For that, I am grateful and willing to give you back this love in return.

I can see now how difficult it must have been to come close to a man who knew nothing about love at all. He knew nothing about how to accept love. He knew nothing about what love looked like. He knew nothing about where to find love. Therefore, when love was staring him in the face, he could not see it. I now understand your words in the past when you said I was hard to reach. I had a lot to learn about how to love a person other than myself. But you were willing to fight for me to get to learn these things and more. You saw that there was some potential inside a man who knew very little of what love was really all about. You loved a person who did not love you in return. You stuck by him with unconditional love until he saw it for himself. I realize what unconditional love means. It is not what I had because I had nothing. It is not because of what I did, because I did nothing. It was not for what I was, because I was nothing. Today I say you are love unconditional.

Anniversary

More times than many, I find myself thinking of you and my babies. I sometimes believe it is these happy thoughts of the family that keep me going. Often without realizing it, a smile appears on my face. I think that if it wasn't for those loving moments we shared, I would have gone out of my mind by now. We are told not to think of the past. But my thoughts are of you and I walking on the beach holding hands. I remember when the kids were babies and you and I looked at them in utter amazement. We were young, and they made us happy in so many ways.

God has been wonderful to me in this short time. I now see the glory of it all. I have a beautiful black queen as my wife, with three precious and adorable children. There are no words to explain the love I feel inside. Happy anniversary I love you Valerie.

Falling in Love

Hello Baby Doll:

How are you and the kids today? Tell them that Daddy is thinking of them and looks forward to seeing them real soon. Valerie, it feels good to know I have your attention and to think you really like hearing from me. I must say, it seems as though something has changed in you. You tend to listen to me when we talk on the phone. Your voice is soft and gentle. Your words are kind and sincere. It truly touches my heart. Am I, for the first time, seriously falling in love with you? Or is it the true effect of what love can be? Whatever it is, please don't stop giving this feeling you give. I won't lose sight of the reason for me being in this recovery program. More than that, I refuse to lose sight of what you mean to me while I am here. I love you still and always will.

The Fear

It had been six months in the Palace, and I had managed to do what was required of me while here. I have worked the twelve-step program, and the talk is buzzed around the house that I must soon exit the program. My counselor Coz kept me informed of the progress I was making and had made during my stay at the Palace. He told me he was proud to be my counselor and to see me work so hard to stay clean.

He commented on me getting my job back and how I had continued to send money home to the family while saving for a rainy day. Coz brought to my attention of his concern regarding my wife not coming to the extended meetings to prepare her and the family for the sober person who was returning home. He was just and fair, showing a genuine concern for me and my family. He told me that those meetings were designed to help her and the family to deal with that different person who had been sober for six months and desired to stay that way. He mentioned she may have moved on, and I may have to do the same while remaining clean. I shook my head as to say I understood.

I got up from my chair as if to leave his office, but only to close the door. I asked if I could speak to him on a more private and personal level.

"Of course," he said.

I sat down. "Having gone through the program and now in my twelfth step, my spiritual awakening is that I don't think I am able to leave the Palace right now," I said. "Yes, I did all that was required, but I am not ready. There is something else. There is more I need to do and more I need to work on. I am afraid and the fear is so great that I feel it in my heart and spirit that now is not the right time for me to exit the Palace."

"Man, you have done everything there is to do," he said. "It is okay to be a little afraid of going back out into the real world."

"That is not it."

"What is it?"

I admired him for his patience and his ability to dig deeper to find the problem and a solution.

I said, "The fear is that I don't ever want to use drugs or alcohol again. The fear is so overwhelming that the mere thought of getting high makes me sick in my stomach. The thought of it all makes me nervous and weak. I am like that trained animal. In a given situation, my body begin to respond negatively. That is the fear of getting high."

Coz listened and thought for a moment. Then he said, "I can allow you to stay for three more months because this is only a yearlong program. In three more months, you will have been here for nine months, and your progress has been great. The next three months will not be easy. The program will be tougher, and I will be much harder and more demanding. I will require more from you to go deeper inside yourself and to pull up all the junk that may affect your sobriety."

Coz was serious about sobriety and the lives of his clients. I knew he understood the problem and the fear I had to face. With tears in my eyes, I nodded in agreement and said, "That will be fine." After regaining my composure, I stood up, said, "Thank you," and left his office.

The Goal

When I left his office, I knew he meant business and I was sure of it. The intensity of remaining in the Palace for three more months mounted. I knew there would be people wondering the reason for my decision. It was simple. I wanted to stay clean. I gave no explanation to anyone. I went on as usual—up early in the morning, going to work, doing my chores, and attending all meetings. When asked to do something, I did it without complaint. I had gotten to where if something needed to be done, I volunteered for the task.

I had narrowed it down to a simple goal: to beat this thing called addiction. It was a point that marked the end of this journey as an addict. My objective was to aim for a life without drugs or alcohol. I worked in the kitchen, washed the dishes, cleaned the bathrooms, and mopped floors. I kept busy. No job was too large, too hard, or too nasty for me. At one point a counselor had asked for a volunteer. When I stepped up, he said, "No, not you. You have done enough." We laughed at that comment.

I took notes in all the meetings, read books on addiction, and prayed every night. My prayer time was a valuable tool and a way to release all the spiritual immoralities that had taken place in my life. I asked for forgiveness, but mainly forgiveness of me turning my back on God. I repented for the time when I lived in the streets and the time when I had contemplated on taking my life. I prayed and became strong in believing that if I would work hard at remaining sober, God would bless my life. In the late hours of the night to the early hours of the morning, I would pray. Besides my own prayers, I would also include a portion of the serenity prayer. I would ask God to give me the strength to change, to accept the things I could not, and the wisdom to know the difference. I had to restructure my life, so I did it in prayer. I outlined my future of providing for my children, going to church, and continuing my education. I knew none of this would be possible without God.

Leaving

The time had arrived when preparations were being made on my day of exiting the Palace. I had scheduled it to be on a Saturday after lunch around two o'clock. When you were about to exit the Palace, the buzz was in the air for weeks before that day. The Palace gave me an exit circle which all the house attended. With me in the center of the circle, everyone took a turn to congratulate, criticize, or advise me on the life outside the walls of the Palace. I thought my wife would have attended, but she didn't. My exit circle went well. Some members of the house spoke with the sound of emotion in their hearts. I was nervous during the entire process, but didn't cry. It was a time to depart, and it was bitter and yet so very sweet.

Once all had been said and the hugs were given, my counselor arranged for someone to take me home, who dropped me off at the curb in front of the house. My kids were playing, but when they saw me they ran to greet me with hugs and kisses.

I asked, "Where is your mother?"

They responded, "She is in the house."

My son Steven Jr. grabbed my bag to help me in the house. When we were all inside, I said, "Just put those things in the room." I told the kids that they could go back out to play while their mother and I talked. When the kids had gone out, she remained in the kitchen, not bothering to show any signs of excitement or gladness. It was okay. I sensed she was not happy with me being there.

She had her back to me while she was facing the sink.

"I managed to save fifteen hundred dollars while in the Palace. I'll give you five hundred for the kids' needs, and we could use another five hundred for the house to catch up on bills and to buy food. The last five hundred we can put into a bank account to start a savings account for the family."

She turned to face me while leaning against the sink. "I think you should give it all to me."

"What?" I spoke in a voice of incomprehension, not understanding what she was saying.

"I think you should give it all to me."

"What are you talking about?"

"I have a jewelry bill that needs to be paid."

"We can arrange to pay it off gradually," I said.

Valerie walked past me, into the bedroom and got on the phone. I was not aware of who she was calling. I waited in the front room, and she came out and handed me the phone, saying, "He wants to talk to you."

"Hello?" I walked into the bedroom to talk. It was some joker on the other end telling me that she owed him fifteen hundred dollars and he wanted all his money. "We can give you a couple hundred and make payments on the rest of the bill."

He raised his voice and said, "I'm coming over to get my money."

"I live here, I will be waiting." I hung up the phone. As I walked from the bedroom to the kitchen, my mind filled with questions. Who was this guy? How did he know I had fifteen hundred dollars? When I had reached the opening to the kitchen, she was at the sink with her back to me. I looked at her for a moment in silence and another question entered my mind. How could she do this to me? I asked, "What are we going to do?"

Valerie turned and said, "If you can't give it all to me, then you can't stay here."

"What?" Again, not understanding what she was saying.

"I said, if you can't give it all to me, then you can't live here."

This time I knew exactly what she was saying. I heard it loud and clear.

The Umbrella

I said, "Okay," and turned toward the front door to leave. As I stepped outside, I saw my children. I motioned to them and said, "Daddy can't stay here."

They asked, "Why?"

"I have to leave you guys again."

We hugged and kissed as the tears flowed. With eyes filled with tears, I wiped my face not to be noticed. With blurry eyes and a brain congested with questions and thoughts, I headed to the liquor store. I had no rational thought of what I was going to do or what had just happened. At that moment of time, my body instinctively responded, and I was on my way. I turned the corner, crossed the street, and entered the store without speaking to the lady at the front counter. I walked straight to the back of the store to the glass liquor case. I could see the different wine coolers and beer through the glass. The glass had condensation on it from the heat outside and the chill inside. I froze in my tracks and stared at the beer and wine case.

For that moment, I could not move, and it was all so very quiet. I don't know if it was a voice in the air or a person who passed by, but I heard it oh so very clearly. It said, "Too many choices." I said, "Hell no," turned and walked back to the front counter then exited the store. I walked across the street to the phone booth and called my counselor Coz. I was crying and trembling with fear. He told me to calm down and to tell him what happened. I told him the whole story from the time I got home to me walking out of the store.

He said, "It hasn't been two hours since you left the Palace. Did you drink or get high?"

"No."

"Where you are?"

"On the corner east of Madison, south of Tweedy."

I heard him in the background, asking if anyone knew where Tweedy Street was in South Gate. He said, "Go over there and pick up Steven right now." He then said to me, "Someone is on their way," and for me not to move. We talked a little longer, and I felt a little better.

Within fifteen minutes, a member of the Palace pulled up in a dark blue pickup truck. It was one of my old roommates. He got out of his truck and greeted me with a hug and said, "Let's go."

By the time we arrived at the Palace, my counselor had arranged for me to live in an extended living apartment until one came available. I was there only two days and on Monday they had moved me to an apartment off of West Century Boulevard near the airport. I was there only for a few months, but while there, little things fell into place. You know the things that stay with you for a long time. One morning, I was walking to the bus stop, and it began raining. I said a small prayer just to myself. "Lord, I need an umbrella." When I got to the corner, it was raining really hard. But just then I looked up and across the street, swinging on the bench, was an umbrella. There was no one around and no one on the bench. I crossed the street, picked up the umbrella, opened it, and it was in perfect condition. This was one of those things that made you think, it made you wonder, and it gave me hope. To this day, I still have that umbrella.

The Effort

It wasn't too long after that I had moved to Altadena and rented a small house. I would pick the kids up and we would spend time at the house and play in the yard. My daughter asked me, "Daddy, why you don't have a girlfriend?"

"You are the girl in my life," I said. Her question told me that her mother may have had a boyfriend or was still dealing with the guy she had.

A few months later, I moved back to Los Angeles near downtown. I had gotten a job in the mail room in a law firm. I was now living in a small bachelor apartment on South Grand Avenue. I was proud of my little apartment, so I asked the kids to come see it. Valerie brought them by, and they said, "It's okay, Daddy. You can make it."

However, Valerie's words to me were, "You don't have shit."

I said, "It's okay. Like the kids said, I will make it."

Once I had gotten situated in my tiny apartment, I worked a second job at night. I would be at the law firm by eight in the morning, off at five, and home by six. I would eat something, sleep, and be at my second job by ten. I would work until six and start the day all over again. I was averaging only four hours of sleep a day. I was told that REM, which is rapid eye movement, is the deepest sleep, but it only lasted for about four hours. I did not want to work myself to death, so on my off nights, I had signed up for a typing class for two nights during the week. The class was Tuesday and Thursday evenings, six to nine and walking distance from my apartment.

It was here when I wrote the Child Support Services to request that I make contributions to my children through their office. I had lost trust in Valerie and felt that all I was doing needed to be recorded and kept by me.

CHAPTER 6

Child Support Service

District Attorney's Office
Family Support Division
5770 S Eastern Ave
Commerce CA 90040

June 4 1997

Steven Mason
1621 S Grand Ave #514
Los Angeles CA 90015
S.S. # xxx-xx-xxxx

Dear Sir/Madam:

This letter is to inform you that I would like to begin paying my family support through your office. In the past I have been sending support directly to the family, which consist of the mother (Valerie White), Valerie Marie Mason age,12, Steven Jr. Mason age 11, Sam Mason age 7. Their address is 125 North Popular Street Monrovia CA 91016.

The amount I can afford each month is $300 dollars. I would like to make 2 payments of $150 dollars twice a month. Please accept this money order of $150 dollars as my first payment for the month of June 97. The second payment will arrive by June 20 1997. Thank you for your help.

Sincerely yours

Steven Mason

Money Orders

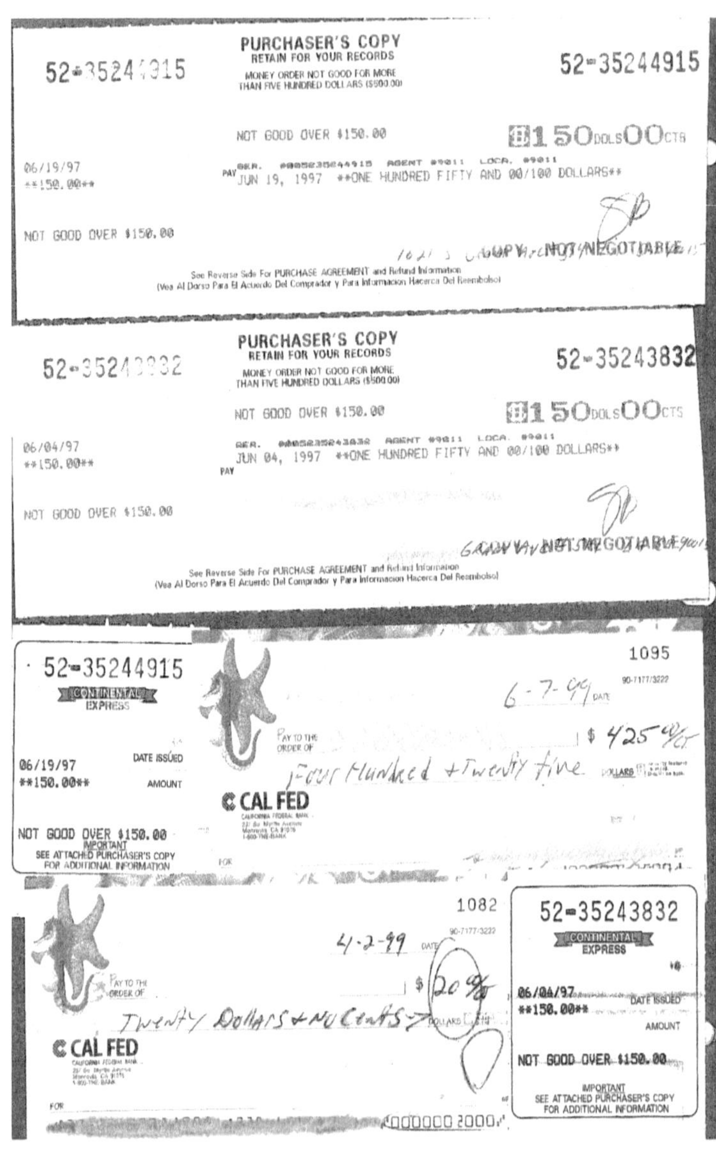

The Response

It was just a page that had two spaces checked off stating that I needed to make the check payable to County of Los Angeles. The response also stated that I needed an identification number or pin number.

BUREAU OF FAMILY SUPPORT OPERATIONS • COURT TRUSTEE

GIL GARCETTI • District Attorney
SANDRA L. BUTTITTA • Chief Deputy District Attorney
MICHAEL E. TRANBARGER • Assistant District Attorney

WAYNE D. DOSS • Director

Date: JUN 12 1997

Dear Payor/Employer:

Check # _______ for $ ______ dated, ______ is being returned to you for the reason(s) below:

________ Damaged upon receipt. Please send a replacement check/money order.

________ Payment must be payable to Court Trustee. Please issue new check.

________ Insufficient information, PIN number and/or case number is required.

________ Payor's full name (as it appears on the court order) and Social Security Number.

________ Authorized signature required on all checks.

________ Please include the Date of Collection, that is, the date the payment was withheld from the employee's earnings.

________ Other: ____

________ Mail all future payments to the following address:

COURT TRUSTEE
P.O. BOX 513544
LOS ANGELES, CA. 90051-1544

Please return your payment in the enclosed envelope with a copy of this letter. If you have any questions regarding this returned item, you may contact our office at (213) 838-7549.

If you have any other concerns you may contact our Customer Service Unit at (213) 838-7550, or the automated 24-hour Voice Response Unit at (800) 615-8858.

PAYMENT PROCESSING

Court Trustee
P. O. Box 513544
Los Angeles, CA 90051 1544
(213) 838-7550

Shadow

One evening on my off night, I walked to the local store for a half gallon of milk. I walked east to Olive Street and headed north. It was a cool night and lit by the full moon above. As I neared the store, I had no thought of anything in particular. I entered the store, got the milk, and was on my way back home. While walking south on Olive Street, I was now facing the moon and noticing how it lit the street before me. As I passed a doorway, I heard a female's voice saying, "Can I have a sip?" The voice was soft, low, and deep-toned, but female just the same. It startled me for a moment. I stopped in my tracks and peered in the dark doorway to see in the rear of the darkness a Black female's face emerging from the shadows. The outline of the face glided out of the darkness as though it floated through a black cloud. I could only see the face and bulging eyes with thin white circles in the eye sockets.

I said, "It's only milk."

"I am thirsty."

I reached into my pocket, pulled out a crumbled bill and some change, and extended my hand in the darkness where it disappeared.

Without touching me, she said, "No," and her face moved ever so slowly backward into the darkness. Within seconds, the face had totally faded and disappeared into the dark as though it had been swallowed by a huge black shadow.

I continued walking south on Olive Street but in my first few steps, my heart filled with sadness. In a low voice, I said, "Lord, have mercy on her and forgive me if I have wronged."

Coerced

One evening, while alone in my apartment, there was a knock at the door. "Who is it?"

A female's voice replied, "It's me."

Curious, I opened the door and, to my surprise, standing there were Valerie and my kids. I let them in. The kids and I exchanged hugs and kisses. They told me they had just come from their grandmother's house.

"That's nice," I said. "Go into the kitchen area while your mother and I talk for a while." I gave them some juice and things that would keep them busy.

I offered Valerie a seat. It was the only armchair I had near the door and at the end of the bed. I sat at the foot of the bed, facing Valerie as she sat in the oversized chair.

"Why are you here?" I asked. She began telling me that after leaving her mother's house, she decided to bring the kids by to see me. "That's nice," I said, "and I am glad to see them, but you should have let me know first." She began speaking, but this time I wasn't listening. I was paying more attention to her. The sound of her voice, the look in her eyes, and her body posture; it was all different. I leaned forward to the edge of the bed and looked her in the face. "He made you have oral sex on him?"

In mid-sentence, she broke out in tears. She lowered her head and sobbed even more. I called the kids and said, "It is time to go."

They began to protest. "Why do we have to leave right now? We just got here and I don't want to go." Steven Jr. asked if he could spend the night.

"We will have to plan for that someday." I opened the door, and we walked down the hall. Valerie lingered a few steps behind as she continued to cry. I talked with the kids to keep their attention and made promises of coming to see them real soon.

When we reached the car, Valerie unlocked the door and told the kids to get in. I hugged and kissed the kids one by one and told them, "I love you and be good."

Valerie wiped her face and, without a word to me, got in the car, started the engine, and drove off.

As I walked back to the apartment building, I thought of how painful that must have been for her. To think a guy loves or cares for you and to find out he only cared for himself. He coerced her to perform oral sex with him. That must have been so humiliating and degrading for her that she would burst out in tears at the moment I mentioned it.

I never made her do anything like that. I always figured we were young and we could grow together.

Once I was driving to work and running a little late, which means I was driving a little over the speed limit. The officer pulled me over and when he walked up to the car I knew I was speeding, so I did not ask, "What's the problem?" He told me that the reason he pulled me over was because I was driving over the allowed speed limit. I told him I was on my way to work and was running a little late, as if it meant any difference to him why I was speeding. He asked to see my driver's license and my registration. Insurance was not a big issue then like it is today, so he did not ask for proof of my automobile insurance. I took my license from my wallet, opened the glove box where I kept the registration, and handed them to him.

He walked back to his patrol car and returned five minutes later. When he arrived at the side of my car, he said, "Mr. Mason, do you know that your license is suspended?"

Surprised, I said. "No. Suspended for what?"

"The County of Los Angeles Child Support has suspended your license. I am not going to give you a ticket, but you need to take care of this right away."

I thanked him. He handed me my driver's license and registration and let me drive away. I thought to myself, *That was decent of him not to give me a ticket. I wonder how many guys he pulls over and they are in a similar situation.*

To get the suspension off my license, I had to go to the child support office, meet their attorney, pay a fee, and make another agreement to meet their standard of child support payments. Then after that, they would give me a piece of paper called a release form for the Department of Motor Vehicles to take the suspension of my license. But before DMV did that, I would have to pay DMV a fee for their service.

The time had come, and I had filed for a divorce. I found a paralegal to assist me with the filing and I paid him his fee. I waited six months and scheduled for the court date. That day came when the judge granted the divorce. I made no special request only to see my children. It has always been my belief to never take the kids from their mother.

I continued to work hard and go to school. The opportunity came when the local college was offering a free computer class. I enrolled in that class and all I had to do was to purchase the book. It was a great introduction class to computers, and I wanted to learn more. After completing my typing class, I enrolled at the community college to pursue an associate's degree. To support myself, I looked for more work. I worked at a local shipping company from five a.m. to eight a.m. Then I would go home for a quick shower and drive to Encino to work in a bank from ten a.m. to four p.m. Return home by five p.m. to eat and be at class by six p.m. This was my schedule, Monday through Friday. On Saturday and Sunday, I drove a truck picking up and making deliveries

COUNTY OF LOS ANGELES
CHILD SUPPORT SERVICES DEPARTMENT

502 FEB 0 3 2003 E4

502 FEB 0 3 2003 E4

DATE: FEBRUARY 03, 2003
Case No.: 020.107.608

Attached below is your copy of the STATE LICENSING MATCH SYSTEM RELEASE FORM that the **Child Support Services Department**   has sent to the DEPARTMENT OF MOTOR VEHICLES CONSOLIDATED PROCESSING AREA.
This release will allow you to renew your license. If you have any questions about renewing your license, please contact:
DEPARTMENT OF MOTOR VEHICLES
CONSOLIDATED PROCESSING AREA.

STATE OF CALIFORNIA-HEALTH AND WELFARE AGENCY   DEPARTMENT OF SOCIAL SERVICES

STATE LICENSING MATCH SYSTEM RELEASE FORM

NONCUSTODIAL PARENT NAME		LOCAL CHILD SUPPORT AGENCY
STANLEY N MASSEY		CHILD SUPPORT SERVICES DEPARTMENT
SOCIAL SECURITY NUMBER	DATE OF BIRTH	2934 E.GARVEY AVE. SOUTH,STE#100 WEST COVINA, CALIFORNIA 91791-2180
LICENSING AGENCY		TELEPHONE NUMBER / OUTSIDE U.S.A
DEPARTMENT OF MOTOR VEHICLES CONSOLIDATED PROCESSING AREA		(800)615-8858 (323)890-9800
LICENSE NUMBER		
U1041157		

This is to inform you that the above named individual is currently in compliance with their judgment or order for support as defined in Family Code 17520.

SIGNED	TITLE	DATE
Rico Oufo	FSO II	02-03-03

CS895REV07.00

for a healthcare company and attended church at six p.m. Sunday evening.

Once I had completed the required courses, I focused my degree in the area of Real Estate. When near completion, I went to a counselor to be certain that I had all the requirements completed for the Associate of Arts in Real Estate. He was impressed with what I had done and suggested that if I take a few more classes in the Mortgage Finance curriculum, I would be able to achieve two associate's degrees. I took his advice and graduated from the community college with not two but three associate of arts degrees.

With no experience, I landed a job as a property manager, making seven dollars and fifty cents an hour. By this time, most of what I earned went to child support for my children. I was living off of four hundred twenty-two dollars a month. You may be thinking that is impossible, but with God and a strict budget, I did it. I applied to the university and was accepted. With the money I had saved from the three jobs, I returned to Valerie to give her four thousand dollars. I offered her this and the chance to take care of our kids without the system of child support service. She was reluctant and disagreed. A few months later, I returned with six thousand dollars in cash. But she refused once again. After that, I focused my attention on the university and what may be ahead.

I was mentally, physically, and financially torn down, but knew to continue to be something for my children. I paid for the class trips for the kids. I took my son shopping for his prom and graduation. I got to see my daughter graduate from high school. The following year, I got to see my son Steven Jr. graduate from high school. Shortly after that, I graduated from the university with a bachelor's degree in Real Estate.

This information is being furnished to the Internal Revenue Service. If you are required to file a tax return, a negligence penalty or other sanction may be imposed on you if this income is taxable and you fail to report it.

Form W-2 Wage and Tax Statement 2004

COMMUNITY DEVELOPMENT COMM
2 CORAL CIRCLE
MONTEREY PARK CA 91755

Box	Description	Amount
1	Wages, tips, other compensation	16275.36
2	Federal income tax withheld	1177.86
5	Medicare wages and tips	18661.40
6	Medicare tax withheld	270.59
12a	G	3088.68
13	Retirement plan	X
14	Other	CASDI 216.87
15	State	CA
16	State wages, tips, etc.	16275.36
17	State income tax	119.32

Copy C For EMPLOYEE'S RECORDS (See Notice to Employee on back of Copy B.)   OMB No. 1545-0008   Dept. of the Treasury - IRS   Visit the IRS website at www.irs.gov.

Form W-2 Wage and Tax Statement 2004

COMMUNITY DEVELOPMENT COMM
2 CORAL CIRCLE
MONTEREY PARK CA 91755

Box	Description	Amount
1	Wages, tips, other compensation	16275.36
2	Federal income tax withheld	1177.86
5	Medicare wages and tips	18661.40
6	Medicare tax withheld	270.59
12a	G	3088.68
13	Retirement plan	X
14	Other	CASDI 216.87
15	State	CA
	Employer's state ID number	801-8271-0
16	State wages, tips, etc.	16275.36
17	State income tax	119.32

Copy 2 To Be Filed With Employee's State, City, or Local Income Tax Return   OMB No. 1545-0008   Dept. of the Treasury - IRS

Community Development Comm
2 Coral Circle
Monterey Park CA 91755

Pay Group:	CDC-CDC Pay Group
Pay Begin Date:	05/14/2005
Pay End Date:	05/27/2005

Business Unit: CDC	
Check #:	0112333
Check Date:	06/02/200

Employee ID:	
Department:	0950-South County
Location:	98SSS
Job Title:	Resident Manager
Pay Rate:	$7.970000 Hourly

TAX DATA:	Federal	CA State
Marital Status:	Single	Single, or Married with t
Allowances:	1	1
Addl. Pct.:		
Addl. Amt.:		

HOURS AND EARNINGS

Description	Rate	Current Hours	Current Earnings	YTD Hours	YTD Earnings
Flex 3 Benefit			220.00		2,420.00
Housing Allowance			95.00		1,045.00
Regular Pay	7.970000	80.00	637.60	852.00	6,726.60
Holiday Pay			0.00	28.00	219.80
Retro Pay			0.00		38.88
Total:		**80.00**	**857.60**	**880.00**	**9,405.28**

TAXES

Description	Current	YTD
Fed Withholdng	36.68	483.68
Fed MED/EE	10.82	118.59
CA Withholdng	3.16	45.43
CA OASDI/EE	7.85	86.08
Total:	**58.51**	**733.78**

BEFORE-TAX DEDUCTIONS

Description	Current	YTD
Blue Shield HMO	98.55	1,084.05
Delta Dental	28.04	308.44
Vision	3.84	42.24
ICMA Basic	150.00	1,050.00
PERS Retirement	15.94	174.63
Total:	**296.37**	**2,659.36**

AFTER-TAX DEDUCTIONS

Description	Current	YTD
PERS Survivor Benefits	0.93	10.23
Garnishment	240.50	0.00
GARN 1001 Child	0.00	1,661.00
GARN 1002 Child	0.00	984.50
Total:	**241.43**	**2,655.73**

EMPLOYER PAID BENEFITS

Description	Current	YTD
PERS Survivor Benefits	2.35	25.85
ICMA Basic	19.13	208.40
PERS Retirement	28.69	314.33

* Taxable

	TOTAL GROSS	FED TAXABLE GROSS	TOTAL TAXES	TOTAL DEDUCTIONS	NET PAY
Current:	857.60	561.23	58.51	537.80	261.29
YTD:	9,405.28	6,745.92	733.78	5,341.23	3,330.27

	SICK	BANK LVE	ADMN LVE	FLT HOLDY	ANNUAL LVE	EAL	COMP TIME
Str Balance:	22.36	118.70	0.00	0.00	0.00	0.00	0.00
+ Earned:	18.34	36.67	0.00	0.00	0.00	0.00	0.00
- Taken:	0.00	0.00	0.00	0.00	0.00	0.00	0.00
+ Adjusted:	0.00	0.00	0.00	0.00	0.00	0.00	0.00
End Balance:	40.69	155.37	0.00	0.00	0.00	0.00	0.00

NET PAY DISTRIBUTION

Check #0112333	261.29
Total:	261.29

MESSAGE:

Community Development Comm
2 Coral Circle
Monterey Park CA 91755

Pay Group:	CDC-CDC Pay Group
Pay Begin Date:	05/14/2005
Pay End Date:	05/27/2005

Business Unit: CDC
Check #: 0112333
Check Date: 06/02/2005

Employee ID	
Department:	0950-South County
Location:	98SSS
Job Title:	Resident Manager
Pay Rate:	$7.970000 Hourly

TAX DATA:	Federal	CA State
Marital Status:	Single	Single, or Married with t
Allowances:	)	1
Addl. Pct.:		
Addl. Amt.:		

HOURS AND EARNINGS

Description	Rate	Current Hours	Current Earnings	YTD Hours	YTD Earnings
Flex 3 Benefit			220.00		2,420.00
Housing Allowance			95.00		1,045.00
Regular Pay	7.970000	80.00	637.60	852.00	6,726.60
Holiday Pay			0.00	28.00	219.80
Retro Pay			0.00		38.88
Total:		80.00	857.60	880.00	9,405.28

TAXES

Description	Current	YTD
Fed Withholdng	36.68	483.68
Fed MED/EE	10.82	118.59
CA Withholdng	3.16	45.43
CA OASDI/EE	7.85	86.08
Total:	58.51	733.78

BEFORE-TAX DEDUCTIONS

Description	Current	YTD
Blue Shield HMO	98.55	1,084.05
Delta Dental	28.04	308.44
Vision	3.84	42.24
ICMA Basic	150.00	1,050.00
PERS Retirement	15.94	174.63
Total:	296.37	2,659.36

AFTER-TAX DEDUCTIONS

Description	Current	YTD
PERS Survivor Benefits	0.93	10.23
Garnishment	240.50	0.00
GARN 1001 Child	0.00	1,661.00
GARN 1002 Child	0.00	984.50
Total:	241.43	2,655.73

EMPLOYER PAID BENEFITS

Description	Current	YTD
PERS Survivor Benefits	2.35	25.85
ICMA Basic	19.13	208.40
PERS Retirement	28.69	314.33

* Taxable

	TOTAL GROSS	FED TAXABLE GROSS	TOTAL TAXES	TOTAL DEDUCTIONS	NET PAY
Current:	857.60	561.23	58.51	537.80	261.29
YTD:	9,405.28	6,745.92	733.78	5,341.23	3,330.27

	SICK	BANK LVE	ADMIN LVE	FLT HOLDY	ANNUAL LVE	EAL	COMP TIME	NET PAY DISTRIBUTION	
Str Balance:	22.36	118.70	0.00	0.00	0.00	0.00	0.00	Check #0112333	261.29
+ Earned:	18.34	36.67	0.00	0.00	0.00	0.00	0.00		
- Taken:	0.00	0.00	0.00	0.00	0.00	0.00	0.00	Total:	261.29
+ Adjusted:	0.00	0.00	0.00	0.00	0.00	0.00	0.00		
End Balance:	40.69	155.37	0.00	0.00	0.00	0.00	0.00		

MESSAGE:

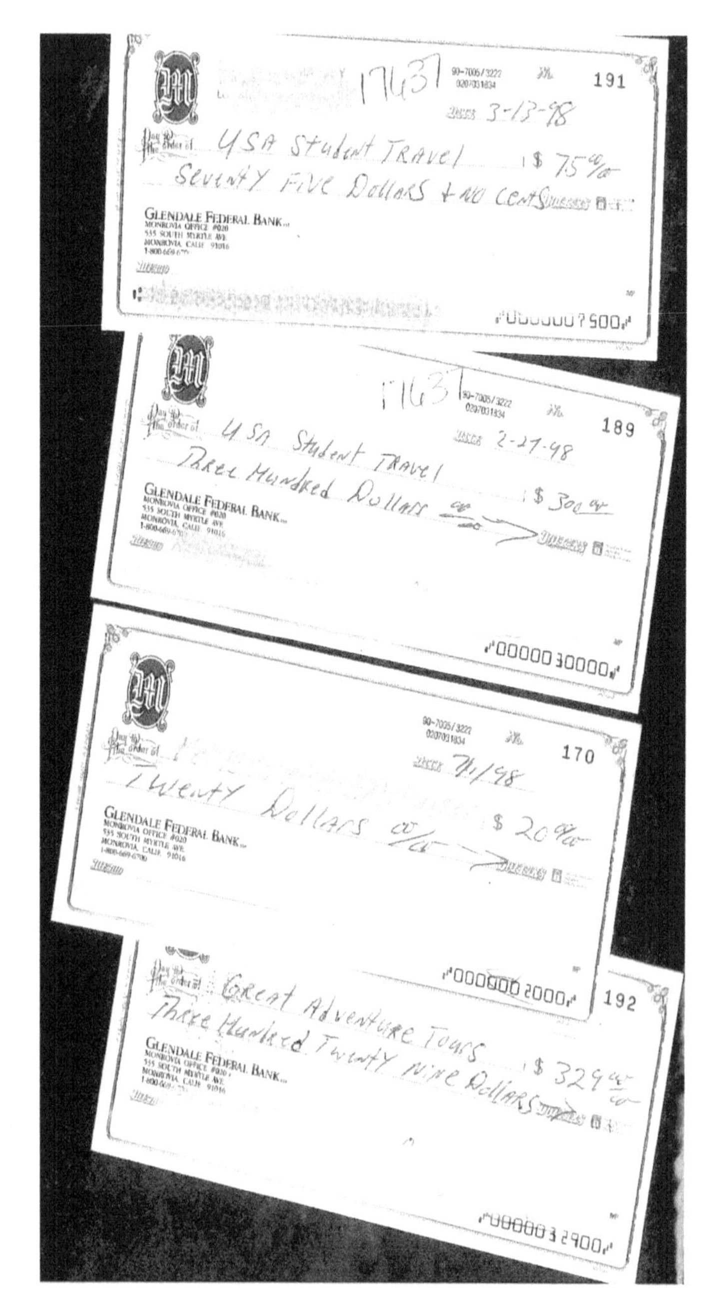

Los Angeles Trade-Technical College

The Los Angeles Community College District
Board of Trustees
on the recommendation of the
Los Angeles Trade-Technical College Faculty
has conferred upon

Stanley Nicholas Massey

the degree of Associate in Arts

Business Administration - Real Estate

Given at Los Angeles, California, this twenty-first day of December, 2000

Georgia L. Mercer *Mark Drummond* *Samuel Castro*
President, Board of Trustees   Chancellor   College President

Los Angeles Trade-Technical College

The Los Angeles Community College District
Board of Trustees
on the recommendation of the
Los Angeles Trade-Technical College Faculty
has conferred upon

Stanley N. Massey

the degree of Associate in Arts

Mortgage Finance

Given at Los Angeles, California, this twenty-fourth day of May, 2001

Georgia L. Mercer
President, Board of Trustees

Mark Drummond
Chancellor

Samuel Casto
College President

Los Angeles Trade-Technical College

The Los Angeles Community College District

Board of Trustees

on the recommendation of the

Los Angeles Trade-Technical College Faculty

has conferred upon

Stanley Nicholas Massey

the degree of Associate in Arts

Liberal Arts

Given at Los Angeles, California, this thirtieth day of May, 2002

President, Board of Trustees

Chancellor

College President

California State University, Los Angeles

The Trustees of The California State University

on recommendation of the faculty

have conferred upon

Stanley Nicholas Massey

the degree of

Bachelor of Science

in

Business Administration

Option: Real Estate

with all the rights and privileges thereto pertaining.

Given at Los Angeles on this tenth day of December, two thousand and five.

Governor
President of the Trustees

Chancellor
The California State University

Chair
The Board of Trustees

President
California State University, Los Angeles

Unemployed

It would be nice if I could say that after getting my bachelor's degree everything was great, but I can't say that. Shortly after getting my degree, I got laid off from my job. It was a hard blow, and I was faced with looking for a job while trying to pay bills on an unemployment check. As you know, unemployment is not enough to live off of. It is only enough to make you go get another job and do it in a hurry. There is another thing you must understand about being unemployed and owing child support. Child support will take a percentage of your unemployment benefits and then send you the remainder.

It would be almost an entire year of being unemployed before finding a job as a Houser Locator. I basically would locate available apartments for families that became homeless for one reason or another. I would contact property managers and owners, negotiate contracts, and place the client in the unit.

My youngest son Sam will graduate in a few years, so I thought. The time came when I expected Sam to graduate from high school. One day, Sam and I were together. I said, "Sam, you will be graduating this year."

He replied, "No, I graduate next year."

"You are a few years younger than Steven Junior, and I calculate that you should be ready to graduate this year. So tell me why you are not graduating this year."

STANLEY MASSEY

1092   CLAIM EXPIRES   SSA# / WEEK PAID   01-05-08 $240.00
10-18-08

BENEFITS ARE REDUCED BY $80.00. THIS AMOUNT WILL BE FORWARDED TO LOS ANGELES
COUNTY TO OFFSET YOUR UNMET SUPPORT OBLIGATION.
YOUR CLAIM BALANCE AFTER THIS PAYMENT IS $4079.00
UNEMPLOYMENT COMPENSATION IS TAXABLE. A QUESTION ON THE CLAIM FORM ALLOWS YOU TO REQUEST
FEDERAL INCOME TAX WITHHOLDING AT 10% OF YOUR PAYABLE AMOUNT. YOU MAKE A NEW WITHHOLDING
CHOICE ON EACH CLAIM FORM YOU SUBMIT.

ALLOW 10 DAYS FOR DELIVERY OF CHECK.   DETACH THIS STUB FOR YOUR RECORD   24230

CONTINUED CLAIM

10-21-07   11755277160710210801120000002080120   A

ANSWER ALL QUESTIONS. SEE SECTION A. ON BACK FOR EXAMPLES
OF HOW TO COMPLETE YOUR ANSWERS. Each question is explained
in your booklet, A Guide to Benefits and Employment Services.

COMPLETE AND MAIL THIS FORM ON   01-20-08

	1ST WEEK		2ND WEEK	
	Begins 01-06-08 Ends 01-12-08		Begins 01-13-08 Ends 01-19-08	
	YES	NO	YES	NO
1. Were you too sick or injured to work?	☐	☐	☐	☐
If yes, enter the number of days (1 through 7) you were unable to work.		(1 - 7)		(1 - 7)
2. Was there any reason (other than sickness or injury) that you could not have accepted full time work each workday?	☐	☐	☐	☐
3. Did you look for work? ☐ <--- IF MARKED 'X', YOU MUST COMPLETE SEC. B., WORK-SEARCH RECORD, ON REVERSE.	☐	☐	☐	☐
4. Did you refuse any work?	☐	☐	☐	☐
5. Did you begin attending any kind of school or training?	☐	☐	☐	☐
6. Did you work or earn any money, WHETHER YOU WERE PAID OR NOT? (If yes, you MUST COMPLETE items a. and b. below)	☐	☐	☐	☐

a. Enter earnings before deductions here ....> $ ________ $ ________
b. Report employment or 'source' of earnings information below:

	DATE LAST WORKED	TOTAL HOURS WORKED	EMPLOYER NAME AND MAILING ADDRESS - INCLUDE ZIP CODE	REASON NO LONGER WORKING (OR WRITE "STILL WORKING")
1ST WEEK				
2ND WEEK				

7. If you want federal income tax withheld for the week(s) shown above, mark this block ....> ☐
8. If you had a change of mailing address or phone number, mark this block and complete Sec. D on reverse ....> ☐

NORCAL AUTHORIZATION CENTER
PO BOX 989057
WEST SACRAMENTO CA   95798-9057

I understand the questions on this form. I know the law provides pena
I make false statements or withhold facts to receive benefits; my answ
true and correct. I declare under penalty of perjury that I am a U.S. ci
national; or an alien in satisfactory immigration status and permitted to
USCIS. I signed this form after the latest date for which I am claiming

X ____________
(your signature is required)

DE 4581-CKOC Rev. 5 (7-07) FLASH   CU-PA662

"Mommy had me repeat the tenth grade because she felt that my grades were not good enough for her."

"But they were passing grades, right?"

"Yes, but she said they were not up to her standards. She said they were not good enough, so she had the school make me repeat that year."

"Why you did not tell me, Sam?"

He had no response, but I knew in my heart why she would do such a thing. She did it only to extend the time that I would have to pay child support. She knew that as long as he was still in high school, she would get child support services to continue to take money out of my paycheck for him.

Shortly after, I petitioned child support services to schedule a court date to modify the case or terminate it because my son was eighteen years old. They sent a simple one-page response that stated they had received my request and it had one line checked off. The second response came, and it was also one page with one line checked off. It had Sam's date of birth, which indicated he was eighteen years old but was still a full-time student in high school, and child support would continue until his graduation in June.

At last, the year had come, and it was Sam's time to do what his brother and sister had done a few years before—graduate from high school. When the time had come, Sam made sure everything was in order. He confirmed that he had taken all the right classes. He made sure his grades were

COUNTY OF LOS ANGELES
Child Support Services Department

STEVEN J. GOLIGHTLY
DIRECTOR

JULY 16, 2008

Dear

In re: Case Name:
     IV-D Case Number:
     LASC Case Number

This quick response is in connection to your recent communication regarding your case. Please be informed that we have:

— Received your correspondence and will conduct a review of the circumstances you have described. You will receive a reply on action taken by this office regarding your concern(s).

— Entered the information you submitted into our database.

— Submitted documents to reinstate the following license(s): _______________________________________

— Referred your case to audit for review. Upon completion, a copy of the results will be provided to you.

— Completed your request to refer your case for criminal prosecution. You will be contacted should we need additional information.

— Initiated necessary steps to convert your order. You will be contacted should we need additional information.

— Initiated necessary steps for a modification review. You will be contacted should we need additional information.

— Investigated the matters which are of concern to you. We will take appropriate action as follows:
____

— Determined that our position is valid despite your comments. It will not be altered absent further order by a court of competent jurisdiction.

— Determined no action is necessary at this time as payments are being made and directed as mandated by applicable law.

— Determined that more information is needed. Please provide the following: _______________________________
____

— Other: ____
____

Very truly yours,

YVONNE HINOJOSA
Child Support Officer

2934 E.GARVEY AVE. SOUTH,STE#100
WEST COVINA , CALIFORNIA 91791-2180
(800)615-8858   32F379
(323)890-9800
Website:http://childsupport.co.la.ca.us

DA041

COUNTY OF LOS ANGELES
Child Support Services Department

STEVEN J. GOLIGHTLY
DIRECTOR

Date: 8/29/07

This quick response is in connection to your recent communication regarding your case. Please be informed that we have:

___ Received your correspondence and will conduct a review of the circumstances you have described. You will receive a reply on action taken by this office regarding your concern(s).

___ Entered the information you submitted into our database.

___ Submitted documents to reinstate the following license(s):

___ Referred your case to audit for review. Upon completion, a copy of the results will be provided to you.

___ Completed your request to refer your case for criminal prosecution. You will be contacted should we need additional information.

___ Initiated necessary steps to convert your order. You will be contacted should we need additional information.

___ Initiated necessary steps for a modification review. You will be contacted should we need additional information.

___ Determined no action is necessary at this time as payments are being made and directed as mandated by applicable law.

___ Determined that more information is needed. Please provide the following:

_X_ Other: Our Records show that the minor child ________ reached age of 18yrs old 7/21/07. However, He is still a full time high school student. Therefore, child support continues until graduation date of 6/30/08 per court order documents.

Thank You,
Yvette Apodaca

Yvette Apodaca

Child Support Officer

2934 East Garvey Avenue South, Suite 100, West Covina, CA 91791-2180 (323) 890-9800
Internet: http://childsupport.co.la.ca.us
"To Enrich Lives Through Effective And Caring Service"

better than good. They were great. He got the suit with the matching hat. He invited the entire family to see him on his big day. It was a wonderful sight to see him walking up to the podium to get his diploma. It was a bittersweet moment for me to see my youngest child graduate from high school and to know he would transition into manhood.

After graduation, we hugged and gave him gifts. I told Sam that I was so very proud of him and I was happy to have him as my son. I expressed great joy, but more importantly, I told him I loved him.

I spoke to his mother, and she said, "Hello, sir." We never say very much, regardless of the occasion.

I hugged and kissed Marie and Steven Junior and told them to enjoy the after-party and dinner with their brother.

I spoke to the kid's grandmother, and she said, "Hello," and complimented me by saying, "You have done a fine job raising my grandson," referring to Steven Jr.

I nodded in agreement and said, "Thank you."

After a few pictures with the kids, I said my goodbyes and was on my way home.

Shortly after Sam's graduation, I petitioned child support services and informed them of Sam's graduating from high school. I also inquired about the application I submitted a year ago to compromise the arrears of child support. The application consists of quite a few pages and your ability to pay the arrears. They asked for proof of my current income, rent, utility bills, and any other expenses I may have. The process is so long because child support services do not respond to an application for at least one year after it has been submitted. They will, of course, send a response stating that they received the application and that it would be considered for review. During the wait process, I worked two full-time jobs. This kept me busy and allowed me to focus on bringing this child support situation to an end.

Child Support Service
Miss Elenor Lee
2934 E. Garvey Ave. South #100
West Covina, CA 91791-2180
Order Number: BD0269041
S.S.: #xxxx

May 18, 2009

Dear Child Support Representative:
I am writing in regard to the compromise application submitted in October 2008.

I have called your call center at (866)901-3212 for the past three months and to no avail all they have told me was to call back. If there is anything you can do to assist in this sensitive situation it would be greatly appreciated. I look forward to hearing from you soon.

Sincerely,
Stanley Massey

CO.   FILE   DEPT.   CLOCK NUMBER   070
ZML   001362   XN50P 0000016897 2

BEYOND SHELTER
1200 WILSHIRE BLVD #600
LOS ANGELES, CA 90017
(213) 252-0772

Taxable Marital Status: Single
Exemptions/Allowances:
   Federal: 1
   CA: 1

Social Security Number:

Earnings Statement   ADP

Period Beginning: 05/16/2009
Period Ending: 05/31/2009
Pay Date: 06/05/2009

Earnings	rate	hours	this period	year to date
Regular	1500.00	86.66	1,500.00	16,500.00
Hol		8.00		
Sick		8.00		
Other				100.00
Gross Pay			**$1,500.00**	16,600.00

Deductions	Statutory	this period	year to date
	Federal Income Tax	-150.60	1,732.08
	Social Security Tax	-99.20	1,029.20
	Medicare Tax	-23.20	240.70
	CA State Income Tax	-40.53	418.87
	CA SUI/SDI Tax	-17.60	182.60
	Other		
	Garnsh	-100.00	
	Insurance	-15.00	
	Adjustment		
	Mileage	+6.55	
	Net Pay	**$1,060.42**	

Other Benefits and Information	this period	total to date
Sick Balance		47.50
Vacation Balanc		119.86

Your federal taxable wages this period are
$1,500.00

STANLEY MASSEY

CO.	FILE	DEPT.	CLOCK	NUMBER	0/0
ZML	001362		XN50P	0000016958	1

BEYOND SHELTER
1200 WILSHIRE BLVD #600
LOS ANGELES, CA 90017
(213) 252-0772

Taxable Marital Status: Single
Exemptions/Allowances:
   Federal: 1
   CA: 1

Social Security Number:

Earnings Statement

Period Beginning:	06/01/2009
Period Ending:	06/15/2009
Pay Date:	06/19/2009

Earnings	rate	hours	this period	year to date
Regular	1500.00	86.66	1,500.00	18,000.00
Sick		8.00		
Other				100.00
Gross Pay			**$1,500.00**	**18,100.00**

Deductions		this period	year to date
Statutory			
Federal Income Tax		-150.60	1,882.68
Social Security Tax		-93.00	1,122.20
Medicare Tax		-21.75	262.45
CA State Income Tax		-40.53	459.40
CA SUI/SDI Tax		-16.50	199.10
Other			
Garnsh		-100.00	
Insurance		-15.00	
Adjustment			
Mileage		+28.10	
Net Pay		**$1,090.72**	

Other Benefits and Information	this period	total to date
Sick Balance		43.50
Vacation Balanc		123.21

Your federal taxable wages this period are
$1,500.00

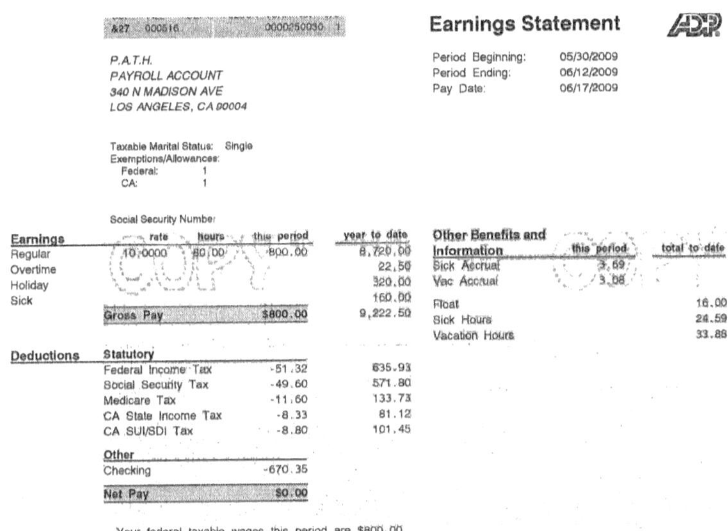

| &27 000516 | 0000250030 1 | **Earnings Statement** | ADP |

P.A.T.H.
PAYROLL ACCOUNT
340 N MADISON AVE
LOS ANGELES, CA 90004

Period Beginning: 05/30/2009
Period Ending: 06/12/2009
Pay Date: 06/17/2009

Taxable Marital Status: Single
Exemptions/Allowances:
  Federal: 1
  CA: 1

Social Security Number:

Earnings	rate	hours	this period	year to date
Regular	10.0000	80.00	800.00	8,720.00
Overtime				22.50
Holiday				320.00
Sick				160.00
Gross Pay			**$800.00**	9,222.50

Deductions	Statutory		
	Federal Income Tax	-51.32	635.93
	Social Security Tax	-49.60	571.80
	Medicare Tax	-11.60	133.73
	CA State Income Tax	-8.33	81.12
	CA SUI/SDI Tax	-8.80	101.45

	Other		
	Checking	-670.35	
	Net Pay	**$0.00**	

Other Benefits and Information	this period	total to date
Sick Accrual	3.69	
Vac Accrual	3.08	
Float		16.00
Sick Hours		24.59
Vacation Hours		33.88

Your federal taxable wages this period are $800.00

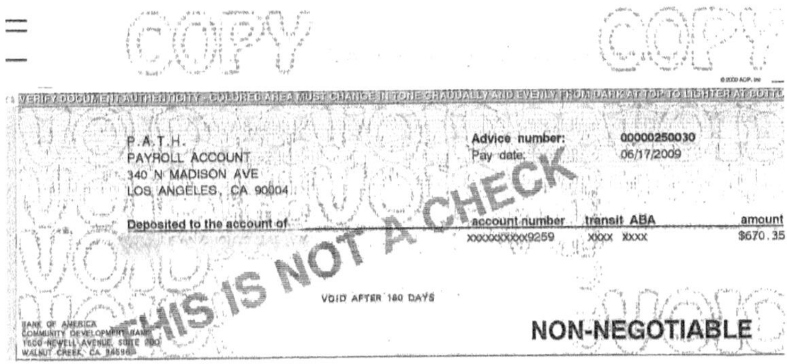

VERIFY DOCUMENT AUTHENTICITY - COLORED AREA MUST CHANGE IN TONE GRADUALLY AND EVENLY FROM DARK AT TOP TO LIGHTER AT BOTTOM

P.A.T.H.
PAYROLL ACCOUNT
340 N MADISON AVE
LOS ANGELES, CA 90004

Advice number: 00000250030
Pay date: 06/17/2009

Deposited to the account of

account number	transit ABA	amount
xxxxxxxxxx9259	xxxx xxxx	$670.35

VOID AFTER 180 DAYS

BANK OF AMERICA
COMMUNITY DEVELOPMENT BANK
1600 NEWELL AVENUE, SUITE 200
WALNUT CREEK, CA 94596

STANLEY MASSEY

P.A.T.H.
PAYROLL ACCOUNT
340 N MADISON AVE
LOS ANGELES, CA 90004

Earnings Statement

ADP

Period Beginning:	05/16/2009
Period Ending:	05/29/2009
Pay Date:	06/03/2009

Taxable Marital Status: Single
Exemptions/Allowances:
  Federal: 1
  CA: 1

Social Security Number: X

Earnings	rate	hours	this period	year to date
Regular	10.0000	64.00	640.00	7,920.00
Holiday	10.0000	8.00	80.00	320.00
Sick	10.0000	8.00	80.00	160.00
Overtime				22.50
Gross Pay			**$800.00**	8,422.50

Deductions	Statutory		
	Federal Income Tax	-51.32	584.61
	Social Security Tax	-49.60	522.20
	Medicare Tax	-11.60	122.13
	CA State Income Tax	-8.33	72.79
	CA SUI/SDI Tax	-8.80	92.65
	Other		
	Checking	-670.35	
	Net Pay	**$0.00**	

Other Benefits and Information	this period	total to date
Sick Accrual	3.69	
Vac Accrual	3.08	
Float		16.00
Sick Hours		20.90
Vacation Hours		30.80

Your federal taxable wages this period are $800.00

P.A.T.H.
PAYROLL ACCOUNT
340 N MADISON AVE
LOS ANGELES, CA 90004

Advice number:	00000230028
Pay date:	06/03/2009

Deposited to the account of

account number	transit ABA	amount
XXXXXXXXXX9259	XXXX XXXX	$670.35

VOID AFTER 180 DAYS

BANK OF AMERICA
COMMUNITY DEVELOPMENT BANK
1500 NEWELL AVENUE, SUITE 200
WALNUT CREEK, CA 94596

NON-NEGOTIABLE

The Compliment Letter

A few months later, I received a letter from Valerie. It was short, complimentary, and it gave me a good feeling when I read it.

Oct 4th 2008

Dear. Stanley,

I just want to say thank you for give me the most wonderful children in the world. And also to say I sorry for everything I have done to you. And never being able to make you happy. And I hope in your heart that you can forgive me. I know you don't ever want to be friends and learn to live with that. Thank you for all the things you have done for the kids its ment a lot to all of them. May God contuine to bless and keep you. And keep up the good work. I will allways love you. In my heart. And you have taught me to love the right way thank you fur that. Bye,

A few weeks later, child support services sent a response stating that it had been determined that I owed Valerie a little over three thousand dollars and some change, and until this is settled first, they cannot continue with the compromise. So this began another process of trying to get Valerie to accept the amount or agree to a lesser amount. I would like to say that it was easy, but it wasn't. She had her way of how the process should go. She wanted me to give her the money and, in return, she would sign a piece of document for me to take back to child support services. I knew this would not work. I told her they would take me through the wringer just to verify that she actually signed the document. I finally convinced her to meet me at the child support office and we could settle the matter in front of them. I did this by telling her she was right and I agreed with her. I did nothing for her and I did nothing for the kids as well. Then I said, no matter what, I will take the money to the child support office, give it to the cashier and she would have to wait to see what they would do from there. She did not like that idea at all and agreed to meet me at the office in the morning by ten a.m.

At five minutes to ten, I arrived at the child support office, checked in, and had a seat in the waiting area. Valerie had not arrived, so my first thought was she was not coming, but my second thought convinced me to wait and that thought was she was usually late. Shortly after ten-thirty, Valerie arrived. She checked in and stood near the cashier's window. A few minutes later, our names were called, and we went into a

STANLEY MASSEY

COUNTY OF LOS ANGELES
Child Support Services Department

STEVEN J. GOLIGHTLY
Director

10/22/2009

Regarding case #

As of today you owe total $7,969.77. Out of this amount, you owe
$3,239.43. You need to pay her off first before you can participate in the Compromise
Of Arrears Program. Please let me know within 30 days if you able to pay that amount
or not. Thank you.

Leo Ton – Child Support Officer

small room. After we were seated, the attorney, a short, skinny African American lady wearing an oversized man's suit, explained the process. She told Valerie that once she signed the form, she could not reopen the case and did she understand.

Valerie said, "Yes," and proceeded to sign the documents.

After Valerie had signed all the forms, I asked the attorney if I could have a copy. She said that I could and as she got up, she said, "I'll be right back." Once she had left the room, I opened my folder and gave Valerie the money orders I had previously made out to her. She looked at them and put them in her purse. When the attorney came back into the room, Valerie got up and left.

I told the attorney that I had submitted an application for the compromise of the arrears and that I would like to continue with that process. She said she would have to submit these forms and put the information in her case notes. She gave me the name of another female attorney along with her phone number and said, "Give her a call. She will handle that portion of the case."

"Is this a working phone number for a real person or just a number for some answering service or machine?"

"It's a real person. Her name is Miss Lee and I will give this information to her and she will contact you.

I said, "Thank you," and left with my copies in my folder.

STANLEY MASSEY

LOS ANGELES COUNTY CSSD - WEST COVINA
2934 E GARVEY AVE S STE 100
WEST COVINA CA 91791-2180

01/25/2010

CSE Case Number
Custodial Party:

Noncustodial Parent:

Court Case Number.

Dear

You have requested our office to close the support case against ⬛⬛⬛⬛⬛ If
you still want to close the case, please complete, sign and date the enclosed Voluntary
Case Closure Request (DCSS 0432) form and return it to:

LOS ANGELES COUNTY CSSD - WEST COVINA
2934 E GARVEY AVE S STE 100
WEST COVINA CA 91791-2180

You may reopen the case at any time in the future as long as support is owed.

Please contact us at (866) 901-3212 with the above case number if you have
any questions.

Sincerely,

DIANNE CABRAL
Child Support Representative

Enclosure

STATE OF CALIFORNIA - HEALTH AND HUMAN SERVICES AGENCY
DEPARTMENT OF CHILD SUPPORT SERVICES

STATE OF CALIFORNIA - HEALTH AND HUMAN SERVICES AGENCY   DEPARTMENT OF CHILD SUPPORT SERVICES

VOLUNTARY CASE CLOSURE REQUEST
DCSS 0432 (09/13/05)

CSE Case Number:

My name is [illegible] I am the custodial party in the support action against [illegible]. The child(ren) listed below is not currently receiving public assistance and no application for public assistance is pending.

The child(ren) in the case is/are:

After considering this matter carefully, I request that LOS ANGELES COUNTY CSSD - WEST COVINA close the case and stop all efforts to establish, enforce, or collect support from STANLEY MASSEY. I understand that LOS ANGELES COUNTY CSSD - WEST COVINA will keep this case open to pursue collection for any amounts that may be owed to LOS ANGELES COUNTY CSSD - WEST COVINA or to the State of California.

I am making this request because _We have come to terms regarding child support._

I certify that I am making this request voluntarily, and I am doing so by my own choice.

I understand that in closing my case I will no longer receive assistance from the Department of Child Support Services to:

- Establish or disestablish paternity.

- Locate the noncustodial parent or any assets of the noncustodial parent.

- Intercept federal or state tax refunds to enforce collection.

- Revoke the noncustodial parent's passport or any business or operating licenses to enforce collection.

- Guide me in enforcing my order or serving documents on the noncustodial parent.

I understand LOS ANGELES COUNTY CSSD - WEST COVINA will no longer be a party to court proceedings regarding this order.

I understand that I may reopen this case at any time in the future as long as current or past due support is owed. However if the child(ren) in this case has emancipated it is possible the case may not be reopened.

PRINT NAME   SIGNATURE OF CUSTODIAL PARTY   DATE

KEEP THIS COPY FOR YOUR RECORDS

UNITED STATES POSTAL SERVICE

CUSTOMER'S RECEIPT

SEE BACK OF THIS RECEIPT FOR IMPORTANT CLAIM INFORMATION

NOT NEGOTIABLE

Pay to

Address

CHild Support

KEEP THIS RECEIPT FOR YOUR RECORDS

Serial Number	Year, Month, Day	Post Office	Amount	Clerk
17750990463	2010-01-23	900171	$750.00	0016

UNITED STATES POSTAL SERVICE

POSTAL MONEY ORDER

Serial Number	Year, Month, Day	Post Office	U.S. Dollars and Cents
17750990463	2010-01-23	900171	$750.00

Amount SEVEN HUNDRED FIFTY DOLLARS & 00¢ ************

Pay to

Clerk 0016

Address

Memo *CHild Support*

© 2008 United States Postal Service. All Rights Reserved.

⑈00000800 2⑈ 17750990463⑈

SEE REVERSE WARNING • NEGOTIABLE ONLY IN THE U.S. AND POSSESSIONS

UNITED STATES POSTAL SERVICE

CUSTOMER'S RECEIPT

SEE BACK OF THIS RECEIPT FOR IMPORTANT CLAIM INFORMATION

NOT NEGOTIABLE

Pay to

Address

CHild Support

KEEP THIS RECEIPT FOR YOUR RECORDS

Serial Number	Year, Month, Day	Post Office	Amount	Clerk
17750990452	2010-01-23	900171	$750.00	0016

UNITED STATES POSTAL SERVICE

POSTAL MONEY ORDER

Serial Number	Year, Month, Day	Post Office	U.S. Dollars and Cents
17750990452	2010-01-23	900171	$750.00

Amount SEVEN HUNDRED FIFTY DOLLARS & 00¢ ************

Pay to

Clerk 0016

Address

Memo *CHild Support*

© 2008 United States Postal Service. All Rights Reserved.

⑈00000800 2⑈ 17750990452⑈

SEE REVERSE WARNING • NEGOTIABLE ONLY IN THE U.S. AND POSSESSIONS

Mr. Tie Called

A week or so later, I arrived home after work a little before five p.m. The phone rang and the person on the other end identified herself as Miss Lee from child support services. She told me that the compromise of my case is being handled by Mr. Leonard Tie and she will need a way for him to contact me. I told her that the best was during the day before four-thirty p.m. on my cell and I gave her my cell phone number. I went on to say that if it was after five p.m., he could call me on my home phone as she had done.

On a Tuesday morning around eleven-thirty, my cell phone rang. It was Leonard Tie from the child support office. He told me the balance that I had to pay to child support and that I would get thirty days to pay it. He went on to say that I would have to agree on the amount and from that date, I would have thirty days to pay the balance. I paused for a moment to figure out my pay schedule and the bills I had to pay.

I asked him, "Can I agree in the middle of this month and pay the balance in the middle of the following month?"

He said, "Yes," then told me he would set the date of agreement for the fifteenth of this month and the final payment would be due on the twentieth of the following month.

A couple of weeks later Adam in the human resource department came to my cubical around four p.m. and gave me a letter on company letterhead stating that child support service sent the company notification informing them they were going to garnish my check for ninety-two dollars and some change starting on the next paycheck.

LOS ANGELES COUNTY CSSD - WEST COVINA
2934 E GARVEY AVE S STE 100
WEST COVINA CA 91791-2180

02/26/2010

PATH
340 N MADISON AVE
LOS ANGELES CA 90004-3504

Your employee:

SSN.
DOB:
CSE Case Number:

Participant Number:

Attention Payroll Department:

Enclosed are the original and one copy of the Income Withholding Order/Notice for Support (IWO) OMB 0970-0154 for each of the employee's cases.

The IWO requires you to deduct a portion of the earnings of the employee and forward this sum to pay a support obligation. To determine the total earnings deductions for support, carefully review the enclosed Summarized Income Withholding Order/Notice for Support (DCSS 0260) as the amount you were previously instructed to withhold may have changed. The IWO commences immediately and will remain in effect until further notice.

As an employer, you are required by law to comply with this notice. If you do not, you may be subject to sanctions or penalties including, but not limited to, those available under California Family Code (FC) Section 5241. This section specifically states that willful failure to comply with the IWO may result in liability for the amount of support not withheld, including interest. This section also states that such conduct by an employer may be punished as contempt of court under California Code of Civil Procedure Section 1218.

You must deduct earnings for support up to the maximum amount authorized by law in situations where the earnings that are subject to withholding are insufficient to satisfy all support obligations. Instructions for handling deductions for support are provided on the back of the IWO. If you do business in the State of California, FC Section 5234 requires you to give a copy of the IWO and Request for Hearing Regarding Earnings Assignment (FL-450) to the employee within 10 days of your receipt of this letter. In addition, you may deduct a fee of 1.50   from the employee's earnings for each payment.

If the employee leaves or terminates employment, you must complete and return the enclosed Termination of Benefits/Employment Notice (DCSS-0114) to the LOS ANGELES County Department of Child Support Services at the address that is printed on the form.

STANLEY MASSEY

INCOME WITHHOLDING FOR SUPPORT

☒ **ORIGINAL INCOME WITHHOLDING ORDER/NOTICE FOR SUPPORT (IWO)**   ☐ **AMENDED IW**
☐ **ONE-TIME ORDER/NOTICE - LUMP SUM PAYMENT**
☐ **TERMINATION of IWO**

Date: 02/26/2010

☒ Child Support Enforcement (CSE) Agency ☐ Court ☐ Attorney ☐ Private Individual/Entity (Check One)

NOTE: If you receive this document from someone other than a State or Tribal Child Support Enforcement agency or a court, a copy of the underlying order that contains a provision authorizing income withholding must be attached. Or if under State law an attorney in that State, or if under Tribal law a Tribal legal representative, may issue an income withholding order, the attorney or Tribal legal representative must include a copy of the State or Tribal law authorizing the attorney or Tribal legal representative to issue an income withholding order.

State/Tribe/Territory ____CALIFORNIA____
City/County/Dist./Tribe ___LOS ANGELES COUNTY CSSD - WEST COVINA___   Case Identifier ____________
Private Individual/Entity ____________   Order Identifier ____________

PATH
Employer/Income Withholder's Name

340 N MADISON AVE
Employer/Income Withholder's Address

LOS ANGELES CA 90004-3504

RE:
Employee/Obligor's Name (Last, First, MI)

Employee/Obligor's Social Security Number (if known)

Custodial Party/Obligee's Name (Last, First, MI)

Employer/Income Withholder's Federal EIN

Child's Name (Last, First, MI)   Child's Birth Date

ORDER INFORMATION: This document is based on the support or withholding order from CALIFORNIA. You are required by law to deduct these amounts from the employee/obligor's income until further notice.

$____0.00____ Per __MONTH__ current child support
$____200.00____ Per __MONTH__ past-due child support - Arrears greater than 12 weeks?   ☐ Yes ☐ No
$____0.00____ Per __MONTH__ current cash medical support
$____0.00____ Per __MONTH__ past-due cash medical support
$____0.00____ Per __MONTH__ current spousal support
$____0.00____ Per __MONTH__ past-due spousal support
$____0.00____ Per __MONTH__ other (must specify) ____________
for a total of $____200.00____ per ____MONTH____ to be forwarded to the payee below.

AMOUNTS TO WITHHOLD: You do not have to vary your pay cycle to be in compliance with the *Order Information*. If your pay cycle does not match the ordered payment cycle, withhold one of the following amounts:

$46.15 per weekly pay period $ 100.00 per semimonthly pay period (twice a month)
$92.30 per biweekly pay period (every two weeks) $ 200.00 per monthly pay period

$________ **ONE-TIME LUMP SUM PAYMENT Do not stop any existing IWO unless you receive a termination order.**

REMITTANCE INFORMATION: If the employee/obligator's principal place of employment is __CALIFORNIA__ ________, you must begin withholding no later than the first pay period that occurs __10__ days after the date of __02/26/2010__. Send payment within __7__ working days of the pay date. If you cannot withhold the full amount of support for any or all orders for this employee/obligor, withhold up to __50__ % of disposable income for all orders. If the employee/obligor's principa place of employment is not CALIFORNIA ________, see the ADDITIONAL INFORMATION FOR EMPLOYERS AND OTHER INCOME WITHHOLDERS for limitations on withholding, applicable time requirements and any allowable employer's fees.

Document Tracking Identifier ____________

OMB 0970-0154

168

Employee/Obligor's Name: _________________ Case Identifier: __________

Order Identifier: _______ BD0269041 _______ Employer's Name: PATH

Arrears greater than 12 weeks? If the *Order Information* does not indicate whether the arrears are greater than 12 weeks, then the employer should calculate the CCPA limit using the lower percentage.

For Tribal orders, you may not withhold more than the amount allowed under the law of the issuing Tribe. For Tribal employers who receive a State order, you may not withhold more than the lesser of the limit set by the law of the jurisdiction in which the employer is located or the maximum amount permitted under section 303(d) of the CCPA (15 U.S.C. 1673 (b)).

Depending upon applicable State law, you may need to take into consideration the amounts paid for health care premiums in determining disposable income and applying appropriate withholding limits.

Additional Information:

____
____
____

NOTIFICATION OF TERMINATION OF EMPLOYMENT: You must promptly notify the Child Support Enforcement agency and/or the person listed below by returning this form to the correspondence address if:

☐ This person has never worked for this employer.

☐ This person no longer works for this employer.

Please provide the following information for the terminated employee:

Termination date: _____________________ Last known phone number: _____________________

Last known home address: ____
____
____

Date final payment made to the State Disbursement Unit or Tribal CSE agency: ____________

Final payment amount: __________ New employer's name: _____________________________
____

New employer's address: ____
____
____

CONTACT INFORMATION

To employer: If the employer/income withholder has any questions, contact __California Department of Child Support Services__ by phone at __(866) 901-3212__, by fax at __(626) 967-6692__, by email or website at: https://www.childsup-connect.ca.gov

Send termination notice and other correspondence to:
LOS ANGELES
2934 E GARVEY AVE S STE 100, WEST COVINA CA 91791-2180

To employee/obligor: If the employee/obligor has any questions, contact HESTER Y LAU ________
_______________ by phone at __(866) 901-3212__, by fax at __(626) 967-6692__, by email or website at: ____

IMPORTANT: The person completing this form is advised that the information may be shared with the employee/obligor.

CHAPTER 7

Wages Garnished

After work, I rushed home to call Miss Lee from the child support office. She answered the phone, and I explained the situation of child support service, indicating that they were going to garnish my paycheck. She said she would check on it and that the information is generated by computer. She explained that the computer did not know that my case was in the compromise stage, so it automatically printed out the garnishment forms and they were signed and mailed. It sounded so logical, but in my mind, I thought that was a bunch of crap. People ran the computer. She went on to say that she would contact me first thing in the morning with her findings.

The next morning, Miss Lee called me at work and informed me she had the termination letter of the garnishment and that she would fax it to me right away. I gave her the company's fax number and waited by the fax machine. A few minutes later, the faxed termination letter came through. I hurried the letter to Adam in the human resource department to stop the process of them taking money from my check. But it was too late because Adam had held the initial child support income withholding notification since February a whole month prior to giving me the letter on the company letterhead, which stated when the garnishment was to take place. By the end of the week, when I got my paycheck, it was garnished for the ninety-two dollars and change.

STANLEY MASSEY

CO.	FILE	DEPT.	CLOCK	NUMBER	070
&27	000516			0094491988	1

P.A.T.H.
PAYROLL ACCOUNT
340 N MADISON AVE
LOS ANGELES, CA 90004

Earnings Statement

ADP

Period Beginning: 03/06/2010
Period Ending: 03/19/2010
Pay Date: 03/26/2010

Taxable Marital Status: Single
Exemptions/Allowances:
  Federal: 1
  CA: 1

LOS ANGELES, CA 90006

Social Security Number:

arnings	rate	hours	this period	year to date
egular	16.8300	80.00	1,346.40	7,135.92
oating Holida				134.64
oliday				403.92
ick				134.64
acation				269.28
Gross Pay			**$1,346.40**	8,078.40

Other Benefits and Information	this period	total to date
Sick Accrual	3.69	
Vac Accrual	3.08	
Float		8.00
Sick Hours		42.39
Vacation Hours		15.48

eductions	Statutory		
	Federal Income Tax	-137.58	825.48
	Social Security Tax	-83.48	500.86
	Medicare Tax	-19.53	117.14
	CA State Income Tax	-39.31	235.86
	CA SUI/SDI Tax	-14.81	88.86
	Other		
	Garnishmnt	-92.30	
	Net Pay	**$959.39**	

Your federal taxable wages this period are
$1,346.40

© 2000 ADP, Inc.

P.A.T.H.
PAYROLL ACCOUNT
340 N MADISON AVE
LOS ANGELES, CA 90004

&27
Payroll check number: 0094491988
Pay date: 03/26/2010

Pay to the order of: **STANLEY NICHOLAS MASSEY**

This amount: NINE HUNDRED FIFTY NINE AND 39/100 DOLLARS

$959.39

ASSISTANCE WITH VERIFICATION AVAILABLE AT 877-423-7243

VOID AFTER 180 DAYS

NK OF AMERICA
MMUNITY DEVELOPMENT BANK
OO NEWELL AVENUE, SUITE 200
LNUT CREEK, CA 94596

ADP AUTHORIZED SIGNATURE

⑆94491988⑆ ⑈121141822⑈ 73130⑉04244⑆

LOS ANGELES COUNTY CSSD - WEST COVINA
2934 E GARVEY AVE S STE 100
WEST COVINA CA 91791-2180

03/24/2010

PATH
340 N MADISON AVE
LOS ANGELES CA 90004-3504

Your employee:

CSE Case Number:
0370020107608
Participant Number:

Attention Payroll Department:

Enclosed are the original and one copy of the Income Withholding Order/Notice for Support (IWO) OMB 0970-0154. This Notice terminates the existing IWO which was previously served on you.

Effective 03/24/2010 you must discontinue deducting money from your employee's wages based on the enclosed IWO. If you do business in the State of California, Family Code Section 5234 requires you to give a copy of this Termination IWO to the employee whose name appears on the assignment within 10 days of your receipt of this letter.

If you have any questions, please visit CustomerConnect on the web, https://www.childsup-connect.ca.gov for assistance on-line or call CustomerConnect at (866) 901-3212. Persons with hearing or speech impairments, please call the TTY number (866) 399-4096.

Sincerely,

HESTER Y LAU
Child Support Representative

Enclosures

NOTICE TO EMPLOYER TERMINATION IWO (COVER)
DCSS 0433 (02/08/08)

STATE OF CALIFORNIA – HEALTH AND HUMAN SERVICES AGENCY
DEPARTMENT OF CHILD SUPPORT SERVICES
ESTABLISHM

INCOME WITHHOLDING FOR SUPPORT

☐ ORIGINAL INCOME WITHHOLDING ORDER/NOTICE FOR SUPPORT (IWO) ☐ AMENDED IWO
☐ ONE-TIME ORDER/NOTICE - LUMP SUM PAYMENT
☒ TERMINATION OF IWO

Date: 03/24/2010

☒ Child Support Enforcement (CSE) Agency ☐ Court ☐ Attorney ☐ Private Individual/Entity (Check One)

NOTE: If you receive this document from someone other than a State or Tribal Child Support Enforcement agency or a court, a copy of the underlying order that contains a provision authorizing income withholding must be attached. Or if under State law an attorney in that State, or if under Tribal law a Tribal legal representative, may issue an income withholding order, the attorney or Tribal legal representative must include a copy of the State or Tribal law authorizing the attorney or Tribal legal representative to issue an income withholding order.

State/Tribe/Territory CALIFORNIA

City/County/Dist./Tribe LOS ANGELES COUNTY CSSD - WEST COVINA
Private Individual/Entity

Case Identifier
Order Identifier

RE:

PATH
Employer/Income Withholder's Name
340 N MADISON AVE
Employer/Income Withholder's Address
LOS ANGELES CA 90004-3504

Obligor's Name (Last, First, MI)

Employee/Obligor's Social Security Number (if known)

Custodial Party/Obligee's Name (Last, First, MI)

Employer/Income Withholder's Federal EIN

Child's Name (Last, First, MI)

Child's Birth Date

ORDER INFORMATION: This document is based on the support or withholding order from __CALIFORNIA__.
You are required by law to deduct these amounts from the employee/obligor's income until further notice.

Amount	Per	Period	Description
$ 0.00	Per	MONTH	current child support
$ 200.00	Per	MONTH	past-due child support - Arrears greater than 12 weeks? ☐ Yes ☐ No
$ 0.00	Per	MONTH	current cash medical support
$ 0.00	Per	MONTH	past-due cash medical support
$ 0.00	Per	MONTH	current spousal support
$ 0.00	Per	MONTH	past-due spousal support
$ 0.00	Per	MONTH	other (must specify)

for a total of $ 200.00 per MONTH to be forwarded to the payee below.

AMOUNTS TO WITHHOLD: You do not have to vary your pay cycle to be in compliance with the Order Information. If your pay cycle does not match the ordered payment cycle, withhold one of the following amounts:

$46.15 per weekly pay period $100.00 per semimonthly pay period (twice a month)
$92.30 per biweekly pay period (every two weeks) $200.00 per monthly pay period

$ __________ ONE-TIME LUMP SUM PAYMENT Do not stop any existing IWO unless you receive a termination order.

REMITTANCE INFORMATION: If the employee/obligor's principal place of employment is __CALIFORNIA__, you must begin withholding no later than the first pay period that occurs __10__ days after the date of __03/24/2010__. Send payment within __7__ working days of the pay date. If you cannot withhold the full amount of support for any or all orders for this employee/obligor, withhold up to __50__ % of disposable income for all orders. If the employee/obligor's principal place of employment is not __CALIFORNIA__, see the ADDITIONAL INFORMATION FOR EMPLOYERS AND OTHER INCOME WITHHOLDERS for limitations on withholding, applicable time requirements and any allowable employer's fees.

OMB 0970-0154

Document Tracking Identifier __________

STATE OF CALIFORNIA-HEALTH AND HUMAN SERVICES AGENCY

DEPARTMENT OF CHILD SUPPORT SERVICES

SUMMARIZED INCOME WITHHOLDING ORDER/NOTICE FOR SUPPORT

DCSS 0260 (02/02/2001)

☐ Original   ☐ Amended   ☒ Termination

Employee Name:

Employee Social Security Number:

Please carefully review the support amounts listed below. The amount you were previously ordered to withhold for the above listed employee may have changed. There may be multiple withholding orders for this employee. Any withholding orders previously sent to you remain in effect, except where a specific Income Withholding Order/Notice for Support is enclosed with an "X" in the termination box.

The amount listed as "Total Monthly Deduction" is the total monthly payment that you must submit for all withholding orders issued for the employee by the local child support agency(ies). The maximum amount you withhold may not exceed 50% of the employee's net disposable earnings unless the court order specifies a higher percentage. The payment cycles provide the total amounts that must be submitted for each pay period, depending upon the wage payment schedule for your company.

Additional instructions are provided on the back of the Income Withholding Order/Notice for Support.

MONTHLY DEDUCTIONS BY CASE

DCSS Case Information	Court Case Number	Current Child Support	Past-due Child Support	Current Spousal Support	Past-due Spousal Support	Current Medical Support	Past-due Medical Support	Other	Total Due
1. CSE CASE NUMBER:	BD0209041	0.00	0.00	0.00	0.00	0.00	0.00	0.00	0.00
2. CSE CASE NUMBER:									
3. CSE CASE NUMBER:									
4. CSE CASE NUMBER:									
5. CSE CASE NUMBER:									
6. CSE CASE NUMBER:									
7. CSE CASE NUMBER:									

TOTAL MONTHLY DEDUCTION:

$ 0.00   per weekly pay period $ 0.00   per semimonthly pay period (twice a month)

$ 0.00   per biweekly pay period (every two weeks) $ 0.00   per monthly pay period

Summarized Income Withholding Order/Notice for Support Additional Page, if attached, includes the support amounts for any additional cases not included in this notice.

ESTABLISHM

The Compromise

Although this caused a small change in my paycheck, I agreed to subtract it from the remaining balance. I set in my mind to pay child support services off by all means necessary. I had one goal, and I was fixed on eliminating this as a problem. Between May third and May sixth, my appointment was scheduled with the child support office to pay the balance on the arrears. That amount was now three thousand one hundred seven dollars and seventy cents. There was only one problem, and that was I did not have all the money required to pay them off. I only had two thousand four hundred dollars. That was all I could afford to pay and be able to survive until another paycheck. But I went with that.

I checked in at the window and waited until my name was called. A few minutes later, an Asian man called my name and pointed to a room for me to enter. He was tall and slender and wearing a gray suit. He was more feminine than the average man. It was more evident when I shook his hand and said, "I am Stanley." He shook my hand with a limp wrist as though he did not want to touch me. I thought to myself, *Finally I see the man whose name I knew on the form he sent.*

We sat down and he got right to the point and asked, "Did you bring the money?"

I told him I did not have all of it, but I had at least twenty-four hundred of it. He said he could accept that amount and would subtract it from the total. He asked if I was going to write a check and I told him I would. I was surprised that he mentioned or asked the method of how I was going to pay by check. It was just a thought for that moment. Then he instructed me to go to the cashier window next door and make the payment. When I returned, he had written the total amount minus the payment, with the new balance on the appointment sheet. He then asked if I could pay the balance in two weeks. I said no, then thought of my pay schedule and how I could live on what I had left. Then I asked if I could have it in a month. He said he could give me until the end of June to pay the balance of seven hundred seven dollars and seventy cents. On a flyer, he wrote the final date before June Thirtieth and the balance amount. Then he gave me a flyer of the location where to mail the final payment and he instructed me to make sure the account number was on the check.

STANLEY MASSEY

COUNTY OF LOS ANGELES
Child Support Services Department

STEVEN J. GOLIGHTLY
Director

March 23, 2010

Los Angeles, CA 90006

Dear

Re: Stanley Massey v. Verletta Whitefield
Court Order Number: BD0269041
Case Number:

This letter is sent in response to your Compromise of Arrears application.

Your application for Compromise of Arrears was approved. Please come in our office between 05/03/2010 to 05/06/2010 to sign the agreement and to make payment of $3,200. You can pay by cash or check (payable to SDU).

Should you have any questions, you can contact us at (866) 901-3212

Very truly yours,

Leo Ton – Child Support Officer

2934 E GARVEY AVE SOUTH 100, WEST COVINA, CA 91791 • (866) 901-3212

"To Enrich Lives Through Effective And Caring Service"

STATE OF CALIFORNIA - HEALTH AND HUMAN SERVICES AGENCY — DEPARTMENT OF CHILD SUPPORT SERVICES

LOCAL PAYMENT RECEIPT

DCSS 0551A (04/08/2008)

RECEIPT NUMBER: 0370074900

DATE: 5/20/2010 10:20AM

COUNTY/OFFICE LOCATION: LOS ANGELES COUNTY CSSD - WEST COVINA

PARTICIPANT'S NAME:

PARTICIPANT'S ID NUMBER:

AMOUNT PAID: $2,400.00

CASE ID NUMBER(S):

PAYMENT MANNER: ☑ Walk-In Payment ☐ Mail-In Payment ☐ Court Payment

PAYMENT SOURCE: NCP-Regular Payment

PAYMENT METHOD: ☐ Cash ☑ Check ☐ Other

PAYMENT INSTRUMENT NUMBER: 1108

REMITTER'S NAME:

REMITTER'S RELATIONSHIP (if other than the noncustodial party):

The date used for applying your support payment to your account(s) will be the date the support payment is received by the State Disbursement Unit (SDU). To have your payment applied to your account(s) quickly and timely, please mail all your future support payments to:

CALIFORNIA STATE DISBURSEMENT UNIT
P.O. Box 989067
WEST SACRAMENTO, CA 95798-9067

If you have any questions regarding this payment, want to sign up for Automatic Payment Withdrawal, or want to make a credit card payment, please call us at (866) 901-3212.

REMITTER'S COPY

LCSA EMPLOYEE ACCEPTING PAYMENT: 19miguelribbon

STANLEY MASSEY

06/14/2010

Participant Number:
Amount Due: 707.70
Debtor:

KINECTA FEDERAL CREDIT UNION
ACCOUNT SERVICES 1440 ROSECRANS AVE
MANHATTAN BCH CA 90266

CHILD SUPPORT COLLECTIONS
ORDER TO WITHHOLD

We are issuing this Order to Withhold to the addressee shown above to collect your past-due child support debt (California Family Code Section 17453 & 17522.5).

This order is directed against any credits or payments belonging to you, and may include:

- Deposits in financial institutions, including Individual Retirement Accounts (IRA) and Simplified Employee Pension Plans (SEP).
- Declared dividends, rents, royalties, deposits in vacation or holiday trust funds.
- Stocks, bonds, mutual funds, etc.
- Any other personal property in your possession or under your control.

If these funds include any money from Social Security or Supplemental Security Income, please contact us immediately at (866) 901-3212.

We instructed the addressee to freeze all credits or payments (up to the amount due) for 10 business days. After the 10 business days, the addressee will remit the funds (including funds from the liquidation of non-cash assets) to our office and we will apply the funds to your past-due account. **Please contact the addressee immediately if you have questions about the liquidation process.**

If the addressee withholds less than the amount due, you must pay the remaining unpaid balance immediately to avoid further collection action. Attach your payment to a copy of this notice and mail it to our office at the address shown above. **Please make your check or money order payable to: Child Support Collections. Include your name and participant number, as shown above on your payment.**

If immediate full payment of the amount due will create an undue hardship, or if you have already paid the amount due, contact us immediately at (866) 901-3212. You have a right to an administrative review.

If you have any questions regarding specific account information or if you disagree with the balance, please call (866) 901-3212 and request the appropriate office(s) listed below.

County	CSE Case No.	Amount Due
LOS ANGELES		707.70

DEBTOR'S COPY

Bank Levy

I collected my things, said thank you, and left the office. It was a wonderful feeling knowing I only had one payment left to pay off child support. I stopped at a local Jamba Juice to get a refreshing juice for the ride back to work. While driving back to work, I thought to myself, *I will not wait until the end of June to make that final payment I will do it as soon as possible.*

On June Fourteenth, I received a notice from my credit union. It stated that there had been a levy placed on my account for back child support. Immediately it came to remembrance of Mr. Tie asking how I was going to make that payment I made on May Twentieth. He knew if I wrote a check, he would have easy access to my account and could do whatever he pleased. I had let my guard down. I had trusted child support services, thinking everything would be alright until I made that final payment. It was quite ironic that child support service would give you time to make the final payment knowing that they were going to do something to jeopardize your ability to do so.

Now I had to deal with the rippling effect of checks bouncing due to insufficient funds in the account. With that also came the charges and penalties of the credit union covering those bounced checks. I also had to call child support services to plead with them to give me a little more time to clear up the mess they caused.

STANLEY MASSEY

KINECTA
FEDERAL CREDIT UNION
P.O. Box 10003
Manhattan Beach, CA 90267-7503
800.854.9846 www.kinecta.org

Notice of Deposit Required

Account Number:
Account ID: 05
Notice Date: **June 29, 2010**

As a courtesy, on June 29, 2010, we honored the item(s) listed below even though the amount exceeded the available funds in your checking account. We value our relationship with you, and are providing this service to ensure that you remain in good standing with the businesses you patronize.

Please make a deposit to your account to cover the overdrawn amount immediately. Be sure to deduct the total amount of the item(s), plus the $29 Non Sufficient Fund per item fee from your check register.

If you would like to discuss overdraft options and additional member services, call us today at **800.854.9846** for more information.

Item(s)	Amount	Status
001111	119.00	Courtesy Pay

Kinecta Federal Credit Union's Courtesy Pay program is a non-contractual courtesy, which is granted at the Credit Union's discretion to checking account holders whose accounts are in good standing. As such, account holders do not have a contractual right to Courtesy Pay. Program terms, conditions, and eligibility may change at any time without notice.

Member Contact Center
800.854.9846

NCUA

Website
www.kinecta.org

1440 Rosecrans Avenue
Manhattan Beach, CA 90266

June 29, 2010

RE: Notice of Levy

Kinecta Federal Credit Union recently received a notice of levy from the following agency:

STATE OF CA - CHILD SUPPORT COLLECTIONS - 866.901.3212

As a result, the following hold has been placed on your account:

$136.84

For more information, please contact the levying officer as soon as possible. Kinecta is obligated to remit the funds to the agency on 07/14/2010.

If you have any questions regarding your Credit Union account, call the Member Contact Center at 800.854.9846, Monday through Friday, 7 a.m. to 7 p.m., and Saturday 9 a.m. to 5 p.m. Pacific Time.

KINECTA FEDERAL CREDIT UNION

Member Contact Center
800.854.9846

Web Site
www.kinecta.org

Final Payment

So on July Twelfth, I wrote the check for the final payment, copied it, and mailed it to the location on the flyer, and I mailed a copy to Mr. Leonard Tie.

Termination Letter

On July Nineteenth, I received a letter from child support services informing me they had terminated support in my case.

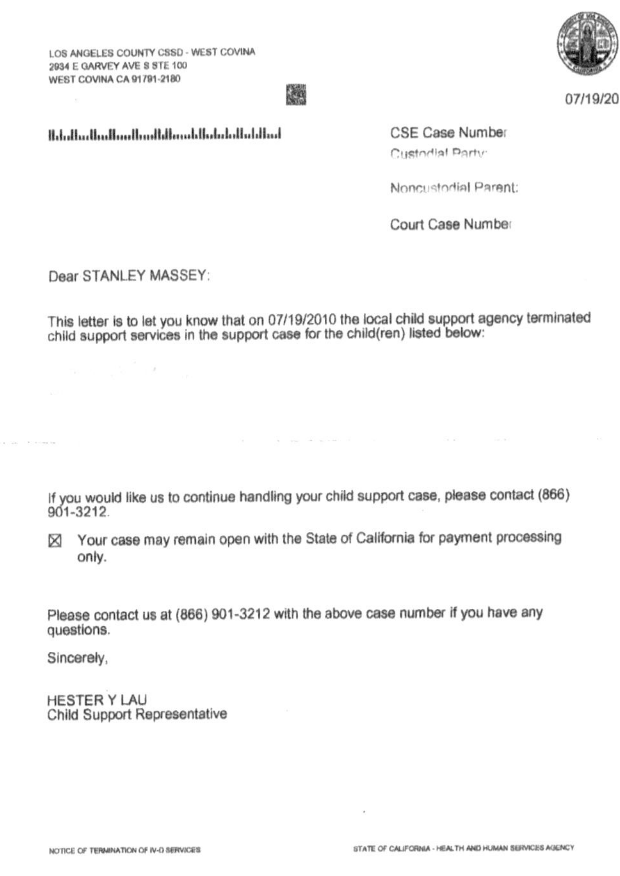

LOS ANGELES COUNTY CSSD - WEST COVINA
2934 E GARVEY AVE S STE 100
WEST COVINA CA 91791-2180

07/19/2010

CSE Case Number
Custodial Party:

Noncustodial Parent:

Court Case Number

Dear STANLEY MASSEY:

This letter is to let you know that on 07/19/2010 the local child support agency terminated child support services in the support case for the child(ren) listed below:

If you would like us to continue handling your child support case, please contact (866) 901-3212.

☒ Your case may remain open with the State of California for payment processing only.

Please contact us at (866) 901-3212 with the above case number if you have any questions.

Sincerely,

HESTER Y LAU
Child Support Representative

NOTICE OF TERMINATION OF IV-D SERVICES   STATE OF CALIFORNIA - HEALTH AND HUMAN SERVICES AGENCY

The Conformation

Finally, I got the confirmation I was waiting for. The check for the one hundred thirty-six dollars and some change arrived in the mail. By this, I knew it was officially over because child support services never sent me a check for any reason.

Due to the number of payments made to child support by court order and the length of the pages, I inserted a few pages to show specific deductions. Those payments and deductions began in June 1997 and went to July 2010. Such deduction consists of voluntary payment, wages garnished, unemployment offset, and tax return.

06

DEPARTMENT OF CHILD SUPPORT SERVICES
CALIFORNIA STATE DISBURSEMENT UNIT
P.O. BOX 989063   01CASWS-000035057633
WEST SACRAMENTO, CA 95798-9063

01102

Pay to Order Of:	
Participant Number:	
Check Number:	0010425115
Check Date:	08/09/2010
Check Amount:	$136.84

According to our records, your support obligation(s) are paid in full or you have remitted monies on a closed case. The payment you have made is being refunded to you. Do not send further payment.

RCPT DATE	COLLECTION RCPT ID	SOURCE	TYPE	CASE ID NUMBER	OBLIGEE NAME	AMOUNT
07232010	9148.0003.00001.00	FTBCSR	REFUND			$ 136.84

Have your payments deposited directly into your bank account. Enroll by going to www.casdu.com or call 1-866-325-1010.

DETACH AND RETAIN THIS STATEMENT
DIRECT QUESTIONS TO: 1-866-325-1010

ORIGINAL CHECK HAS A COLORED BACKGROUND WITH A MICRO PRINTED WARNING BAND

DEPARTMENT OF CHILD SUPPORT SERVICES
CALIFORNIA STATE DISBURSEMENT UNIT
P.O. BOX 989063
WEST SACRAMENTO, CA 95798-9063
1-866-325-1010

11-35
1210 CA

0010425115

August 09, 2010

PAY EXACTLY: ONE HUNDRED THIRTY SIX DOLLARS AND 84 CENTS

TO THE ORDER OF:

$ ******136.84

VOID AFTER 180 DAYS

MEMO:

Bank of America
Bank of America N.A. Sacramento, California

AUTHORIZED SIGNATURE

EXPLANATION OF ADDITIONAL SECURITY FEATURES INDICATED ON REVERSE SIDE

STANLEY MASSEY

2-35244915

52-352449

NOT GOOD OVER $150.00

150 DOLS 00 CT

/97
.00**

PAY SER. #005235244915 AGENT #9011 LOCA. #9011
JUN 19, 1997 **ONE HUNDRED FIFTY AND 00/100 DOLLARS**

OOD OVER $150.00

COPY - NOT NEGOTIABLE

See Reverse Side For PURCHASE AGREEMENT and Refund Information
(Vea Al Dorso Para El Acuerdo Del Comprador y Para Informacion Hacerca Del Reembolso)

PURCHASER'S COPY
RETAIN FOR YOUR RECORDS

2-35243832

52-3524383

NOT GOOD OVER $150.00

150 DOLS 00 CT

/97
.00**

SER. #005235243832 AGENT #9011 LOCA. #9011
JUN 04, 1997 **ONE HUNDRED FIFTY AND 00/100 DOLLARS**
PAY

OOD OVER $150.00

COPY - NOT NEGOTIABLE

See Reverse Side For PURCHASE AGREEMENT and Refund Information
(Vea Al Dorso Para El Acuerdo Del Comprador y Para Informacion Hacerca Del Reembolso)

2-35244915

CONTINENTAL EXPRESS

1095

90-7177/3222

6-7-99 DATE

PAY TO THE ORDER OF

$ 425

Four Hundred + Twenty five DOLLARS

'97
00** DATE ISSUED AMOUNT

CAL FED
CALIFORNIA FEDERAL BANK
937 So. Myrtle Avenue
Monrovia CA 91016
1-800-THE-BANK

OOD OVER $150.00
IMPORTANT
TTACHED PURCHASER'S COPY
ADDITIONAL INFORMATION

FOR

1082

4-2-99 DATE

90-7177/3222

PAY TO THE ORDER OF

$ 20

Twenty Dollars + No Cents DOLLARS

CAL FED
CALIFORNIA FEDERAL BANK
937 So. Myrtle Avenue
Monrovia CA 91016
1-800-THE-BANK

52-35243832

CONTINENTAL EXPRESS

06/04/97 DATE ISSUE
150.00 AMOUN

NOT GOOD OVER $150.00

IMPORTANT
SEE ATTACHED PURCHASER'S COPY
FOR ADDITIONAL INFORMATION

STANLEY MASSEY

COUNTY OF LOS ANGELES
CHILD SUPPORT SERVICES DEPARTMENT

Start Pay Period Q-03.

:Y 03, 2003

IMUNITY DEVLPMT COMMISSION LOS
:ELES COUNTY
:ORAL CIRCLE
ITEREY PARK, CA 91755-

n. Payroll Department

ar Employer:

e:

:losed is an Order/Notice to Withhold Income for Child Support and/or Order for Health Insurance Coverag
:signment) in the above case. Such assignments are required by California law in every case where an order fc
:port is payable through a court designated agency such as the Court Trustee   . The purpose of thi
uirement is to ensure that families receive the support to which they are legally entitled in a timely and regula
nner.

furtherance of this public policy the Code of Federal Regulations and the California Family Code impose specifi
uirements for the payment and distribution of support payments made by earnings assignment. Among othe
igs federal regulations require that the employer send the payment to the payee (in this case, th
irt Trustee   ) within 10 days of the date the money is payable to the employee. In addition federa
ulations require that the funds be applied to the payor's account as if paid on the payroll date on which you
ployee would otherwise have received them (date of collection). It is therefore necessary that the date c
lection be supplied with each earnings assignment payment that you submit on your employee's behalf.

ensure that payments are properly distributed and that your employee gets proper credit, please supply all c
following information for each earnings assignment payment you submit:

1. **Date of Collection**
2. **Case Number**
3. **Last Name, First Name (as they appear on court order)**

ke payments payable and mail to:
IURT TRUSTEE, P.O. BOX 513544, LOS ANGELES, CA 90051-1544

ditional information about the Order/Notice to Withhold Income for Child Support is contained on the revers
e of the Order/Notice to Withhold Income for Child Support.

ur assistance and cooperation are appreciated. Please do not hesitate to call if there are any questions.

ry truly yours,

NTHIA A. WILLIAMS
nily Support Officer

:losure

2934 E.GARVEY AVE. SOUTH,STE#1(
WEST COVINA, CALIFORNIA 91791-21£
(323)890-9800, 31F3(
Outside USA   (323)890-98(
Website:http://childsupport.co.la.ca.ı

:SREV03.02

⌐ Original |X| Amended |_| Termination

te CALIFORNIA
/City/Dist. Of LOS ANGELES
ꞁunal/Case Number ▮▮▮▮▮▮

⌐MUNITY DEVLPMT COMMISSION LOS
Employer/Withholder's Name
ꞳELES COUNTY
Employer/Withholder's Address
ꞳORAL CIRCLE
ꞁTEREY PARK, CA 91755

Employer/Withholder's Federal EIN Number (if known)	Child(ren)'s Name(s):	DOB
▮▮▮▮▮▮	▮▮▮▮▮▮	

Employee/Obligor's Name (Last, First, MI)
▮▮▮▮▮▮

Employee/Obligor's Social Security Number
▮▮▮▮▮▮

Employee/Obligor's Case Identifier

▮▮▮▮▮▮

Obligee's Name (Last, First, MI)

⌐| If checked, you are required to enroll the child(ren) identified above in any health insurance coverage available t⌐
ployee/obligor through his/her employment.

DER INFORMATION: This *Order/Notice* is based upon an order for support order ▮▮▮▮▮▮ from CALIFORNIA
ꞁ are required by law to deduct these amounts from employee's/obligor's income until further notice.

42.00	Per MONTH	current child support
79.00	Per MONTH	past-due child support–Arrears 12 weeks or greater? ⌐ yes |X| no
	Per	current medical support
	Per	past-due medical support
	Per	spousal support
	Per	other (specify):

a total of $621.00   per MONTH   to be forwarded to the payee below.

ꞁ do not have to vary your pay cycle to be in compliance with the support order. If your pay cycle does not match the or
ꞁment cycle, use the following to determine how much to withhold:

43.41   per weekly pay period. $310.50   per semimonthly pay period (twice a month).
36.17   per biweekly pay period (every two weeks). $621.00   per monthly pay period.

MITTANCE INFORMATION: When remitting payment, provide the paydate/date of withholding and the case identifier. If the
ployee's/obligor's principal place of employment is CA _______, begin withholding no later than the first pay p
ꞁurring 10 days after the date of this *Order/Notice*. Send payment within 7 working days of the paydate/date of
ꞁhholding. The total withheld amount, including your fee, cannot exceed 50 % of the employee's/obligor's aggregate dispos
ekly earnings.

he employee's/obligor's principal place of employment is not CA _______, for limitations on withholding, appli⌐
ꞁe requirements, and any allowable employer fees, follow the laws and procedures of the employee's/obligor's principal place
ployment (see #4 and #10, ADDITIONAL INFORMATION TO EMPLOYERS AND OTHER WITHHOLDERS).

emitting payment by EFT/EDI, call (323) 838-7500 before first submission. Use this FIPS code: 06037
ꞁk routing code: _______   Bank account number: _______.

ke check payable to: *(Payee and Case identifier):* COURT TRUSTEE ▮▮▮▮▮▮
ꞁd check to: P.O. BOX 513544
LOS ANGELES, CA 90051

thorized by:	_(signature)_	Date: JULY 03, 2003
thorized by:		Date:
ꞁt Name	LORI A. CRUZ, CHIEF ATTORNEY	Date:
Authorized		Date:
ꞁicial(s):		Date:

ꞁPORTANT: The person completing this form is advised that the information on this form may be shared with the obligor.

STANLEY MASSEY

Original	☐ Amended	☐ Termination

ɔ CALIFORNIA
City/Dist. Of LOS ANGELES
ınal/Case Number ████████

REALTY MANAGEMENT   INC
Employer/Withholder's Name
ł TOPANGA CANYON BLVD STE 210
Employer/Withholder's Address
ƆGA PARK, CA 91303-1251

⸻

ʔ05738
Employer/Withholder's Federal EIN Number (if known)

████████
Employee/Obligor's Name (Last, First, MI)

████████
Employee/Obligor's Social Security Number

████████
Employee/Obligor's Case Identifier

████████
Obligee's Name (Last, First, MI)

Child(ren)'s Name(s):   ████████   DOB 07/21/198

☐ If checked, you are required to enroll the child(ren) identified above in any health insurance coverage available to loyee/obligor through his/her employment.

ER INFORMATION: This *Order/Notice* is based upon an order for support order ████████ from **CALIFORNIA** . ɘ are required by law to deduct these amounts from employee's/obligor's income until further notice.

?.00	Per MONTH	current child support
?.00	Per MONTH	past-due child support–Arrears 12 weeks or greater? ☒ yes ☐ no
	Per	current medical support
	Per	past-due medical support
	Per	spousal support
	Per	other (specify):

ɔ total of $481.00   per MONTH   to be forwarded to the payee below.

do not have to vary your pay cycle to be in compliance with the support order. If your pay cycle does not match the ordɐ nent cycle, use the following to determine how much to withhold:

L.08	per weekly pay period.	$240.50	per semimonthly pay period (twice a month).
L.65	per biweekly pay period (every two weeks).	$481.00	per monthly pay period.

ITTANCE INFORMATION: When remitting payment, provide the paydate/date of withholding and the case identifier. If the loyee's/obligor's principal place of employment is **CALIFORNIA** , begin withholding no later than the first pay per rring 10 days after the date of this *Order/Notice*. Send payment within 7 working days of the paydate/date of holding. The total withheld amount, including your fee, cannot exceed 50 % of the employee's/obligor's aggregate disposa ɗy earnings.

ɘ employee's/obligor's principal place of employment is not **CALIFORNIA** , for limitations on withholding, applica requirements, and any allowable employer fees, follow the laws and procedures of the employee's/obligor's principal place ɔ ɔyment (see #4 and #10, ADDITIONAL INFORMATION TO EMPLOYERS AND OTHER WITHHOLDERS).

nitting payment by EFT/EDI, call (866) 325-1010 before first submission. Use this FIPS code: 06037
ɔ routing code: _______________ Bank account number: _______________ .

ɘ check payable to: *(Payee and Case Identifier):* STATE DISBURSEMENT ████████
ɩ check to: P.O. BOX 989067
WEST SACRAMENTO, CA 95798

ɔorized by: *(signature)*	Date: JUNE 10, 2007
ɔorized by:	Date:
Name LORI A. CRUZ, CHIEF ATTORNEY	Date:
uthorized	Date:
ɩal(s):	Date:

ƆRTANT: The person completing this form is advised that the information on this form may be shared with the obligor.

03183292-00004531

```
tS129                    AP  PAYMENT HISTORY              MBONILLA 20080729

) NAME: [REDACTED]                              PIN: 04.3020.2758 PAGE
:CEIPT DATE:                     PAYMENT SOURCE:          REVERSE VIEW:

COLL DATE RCPT DATE POST DATE BATCH/RECEIPT #     SOURCE AMOUNT     COMMEN1

 20080724  20080724  20080725 080724-8802-061000 WGA        240.50
 20080714  20080714  20080715 080714-8802-016000 WGA        240.50
 20080624  20080624  20080625 080624-8806-580000 WGA        240.50
 20080610  20080610  20080611 080610-8809-911000 WGA        240.50
 20080530  20080530  20080531 080530-8801-099000 WGA        240.50
 20080512  20080512  20080513 080512-8801-339000 WGA        240.50
 20080424  20080424  20080425 080424-8803-993000 WGA        240.50
 20080115  20080115  20080116 080115-9601-080000 UIB         80.00
 20080115  20080115  20080116 080115-9601-079000 UIB         80.00
 20080102  20080102  20080103 080102-9601-073000 UIB         80.00
 20080102  20080102  20080103 080102-9601-074000 UIB         80.00
 20071218  20071218  20071219 071218-9601-079000 UIB         80.00
 20071218  20071218  20071219 071218-9601-078000 UIB         80.00
                                                          2163.50 ** Mo1
'1    F2    F3    F4    F5      F6    F7    F8    F9   F10      F11      I
'PH01    PFPH01    S01290    DFPH1291 DFPH1292  55   55  06037   19
tow: 04 Col: 59 NFPH  Use ALT key or Mouse to access Menu Accelerators
```

36988. 28

179 x 72 = 1288

179 x 6 years

```
3129                    AP PAYMENT HISTORY              MBONILLA 20080729   ]

 NAME: ██████████████              PIN: 04.3020.2758 PAGE:
 :EIPT DATE:                PAYMENT SOURCE:      REVERSE VIEW:

:OLL DATE RCPT DATE POST DATE BATCH/RECEIPT #    SOURCE AMOUNT      COMMENT

 20071204  20071204  20071205 071204-9601-087000 UIB       80.00
 20071204  20071204  20071205 071204-9601-088000 UIB       80.00
 20071120  20071120  20071121 071120-9601-079000 UIB       80.00
 20071120  20071120  20071121 071120-9601-078000 UIB       80.00
 20071106  20071106  20071107 071106-9601-080000 UIB       80.00
 20070924  20070924  20070925 070924-8809-810000 WGA      240.50
 20070910  20070910  20070911 070910-8803-370000 WGA      240.50
 20070823  20070823  20070824 070823-8801-094000 WGA      240.50
 20070809  20070809  20070810 070809-8803-705000 WGA      240.50
 20070723  20070723  20070724 070723-8804-058000 WGA      240.50
 20070709  20070709  20070710 070709-8807-062000 WGA      240.50
 20070508  20070508  20070509 070508-9601-087000 UIB       86.00
 20070501  20070501  20070503 070501-9601-063000 UIB       86.00
                                                           ** More
   .    F2     F3     F4     F5     F6     F7    F8    F9   F10    F11      F1
 PH01    PFPH01     S01290   DFPH1291  DFPH1292  55   55   06037  19
 :w: 04 Col: 59 NFPH  Use ALT key or Mouse to access Menu Accelerators
```

2015

```
RS129                    AP PAYMENT HISTORY              MBONILLA 20080729

? NAME: ███████████████              PIN: 04.3020.2758 PAGI
RCEIPT DATE:               PAYMENT SOURCE:      REVERSE VIEW:

COLL DATE RCPT DATE POST DATE BATCH/RECEIPT #   SOURCE AMOUNT      COMMEN

 20060929  20060929  20060930 060929-8801-577000 WGA       221.65
 20060914  20060914  20060915 060914-8802-935000 WGA       221.65
 20060831  20060831  20060901 060831-8803-045000 WGA       221.65
 20060818  20060818  20060819 060818-8801-791000 WGA       221.65
 20060803  20060803  20060804 060803-8802-175000 WGA       221.65
 20060721  20060721  20060722 060721-8901-002000 WRT       221.65
 20060707  20060707  20060708 060707-8501-046000 URI       221.65
 20060623  20060623  20060624 060623-8801-584000 WGA       221.65
 20060609  20060609  20060610 060609-8805-452000 WGA       221.65
 20060526  20060526  20060527 060526-8803-224000 WGA       221.65
 20060512  20060512  20060513 060512-9103-312000 IRS     1,560.91
 20060512  20060512  20060513 060512-8801-964000 WGA       221.65
 20050120  20050203  20060505 050203-9102-139101 IRS      -276.00 IRS NE(
                                                              ** Mo1
F1    F2    F3    F4     F5     F6     F7    F8    F9   F10    F11      1
FPH01   PFPH01   S01290   DFPH1291  DFPH1292  55  55  06037  19
Row: 04 Col: 59 NFPH  Use ALT key or Mouse to access Menu Accelerators
```

```
RS129                    AP PAYMENT HISTORY            MBONILLA 20080729

? NAME: ███████████████            PIN: 04.3020.2758 PAGE
CEIPT DATE:                      PAYMENT SOURCE:       REVERSE VIEW:

COLL DATE RCPT DATE POST DATE BATCH/RECEIPT #    SOURCE AMOUNT      COMMENT

 20050120  20050203  20060504 050203-9102-139101 IRS      276.00 IRS NEC
 20050120  20050203  20060504 050203-9102-139102 IRS      219.15
 20050120  20050203  20060504 050203-9102-139000 IRS     -495.15 SUSPENS
 20060421  20060428  20060428 060428-0038-041000 WGA      221.65
 20060412  20060418  20060419 060419-0083-064000 WGA      221.65
 20060329  20060403  20060403 060403-0039-094000 WGA      221.65
 20060217  20060301  20060302 060301-0801-014000 WGA      443.30
 20060131  20060209  20060209 060209-0086-021000 WGA      443.30
 20051229  20060104  20060106 060106-0001-044000 WGA      443.30
 20051130  20051212  20051213 051213-0005-023000 WGA      443.30
 20051028  20051108  20051110 051110-0076-042000 WGA      443.30
 20050928  20050930  20051014 050930-0060-013100 WGA      664.95
 20050712  20050712  20050712 050712-0057-024000 REG      302.00
                                                                  ** MO
F1    F2    F3    F4     F5      F6    F7    F8    F9   F10    F11     1
FPH01    PFPH01    S01290    DFPH1291  DFPH1292 55   55   06037 19
Row: 04 Col: 59 NFPH  Use ALT key or Mouse to access Menu Accelerators
```

FRANCHISE TAX BOARD
PO BOX 942840
SACRAMENTO CA 94240

581800110099

05/12/05

RETURN INFORMATION NOTICE

☐ Check this box and indicate new address on reverse.

Account Number: ▮▮▮▮▮▮

Tax Year: 2004
SSAN: ▮▮▮▮▮▮

Balance: $ 0.00

KEEP THIS NOTICE FOR YOUR RECORDS.

NOTICE ID: ▮▮▮▮▮▮   ACCOUNT NUMBER: ▮▮▮▮▮▮

04 Tax Year Summary

Taxable income	$	9,707.00
Tax	$	97.00
Exemptions	$	-350.00
Total tax liability	$	0.00
Interest allowed	$	-0.05
Withholding	$	-119.00
Applied to balance due	$	88.42
Applied per agency offset request	$	30.63
Revised balance	$	0.00

The balance for this tax year reflects all payments or credits applied to your account through 05/07/05. We did not include balances for other tax years in this notice. If you have a balance on another tax year, we will send a separate billing.

Explanation of Revisions

We revised your California state income tax return for the 2004 tax year. The information below explains why we made the revisions:

You owed money to a government agency, which may include us. We applied the refund from your return to that liability.

We applied the overpayment on your return to another tax year or a taxpayer penalty on your account.

For Additional Information

For more information regarding these revisions, go to our Website at www.ftb.ca.gov, search for: Notice Code, and select the following codes: 02 04.

See the enclosed insert for more information about penalties, interest, and your rights as a California taxpayer.

818A MEO (REV 08-2002)

STANLEY MASSEY

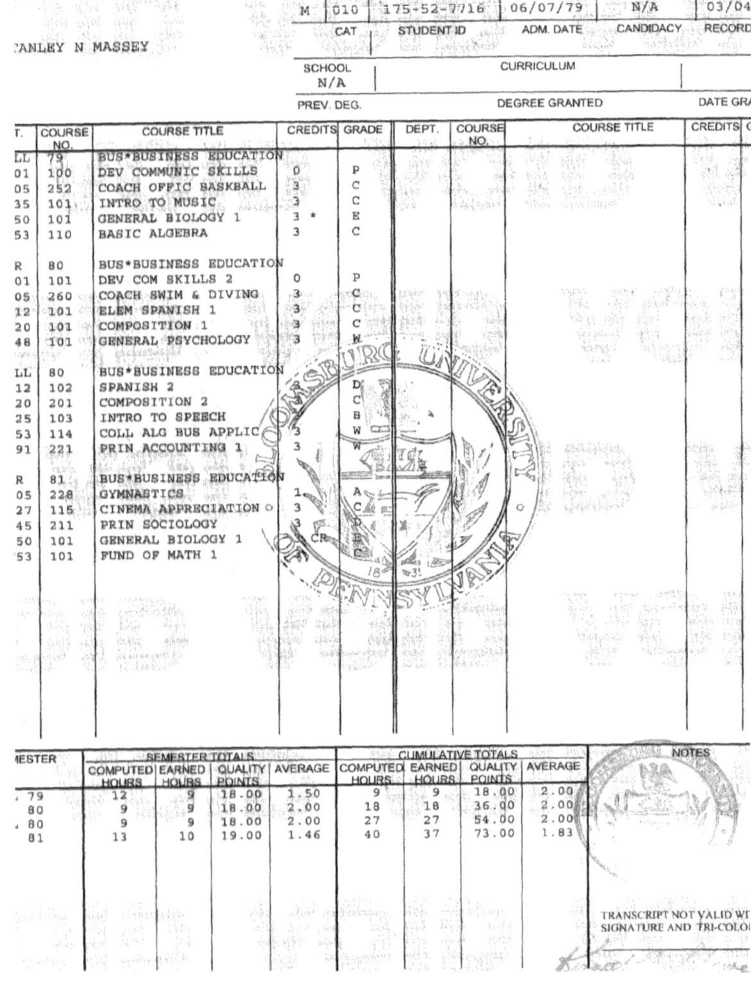

BLOOMSBURG UNIVERSITY OF PENNSYLVANIA
BLOOMSBURG, PENNSYLVANIA

ACADEMIC RECORD
PAGE 1 OF 1

:ANLEY N MASSEY

	M	010	175-52-7716	06/07/79	N/A	03/04
		CAT	STUDENT ID	ADM. DATE	CANDIDACY	RECORD

SCHOOL N/A	CURRICULUM	
PREV. DEG.	DEGREE GRANTED	DATE GR/

T.	COURSE NO.	COURSE TITLE	CREDITS	GRADE	DEPT.	COURSE NO.	COURSE TITLE	CREDITS G
LL	79	BUS*BUSINESS EDUCATION						
01	100	DEV COMMUNIC SKILLS	0	P				
05	252	COACH OFFIC BASKBALL	3	C				
35	101	INTRO TO MUSIC	3	C				
50	101	GENERAL BIOLOGY 1	3 *	E				
53	110	BASIC ALGEBRA	3	C				
R	80	BUS*BUSINESS EDUCATION						
01	101	DEV COM SKILLS 2	0	P				
05	260	COACH SWIM & DIVING	3	C				
12	101	ELEM SPANISH 1	3	C				
20	101	COMPOSITION 1	3	C				
48	101	GENERAL PSYCHOLOGY	3	W				
LL	80	BUS*BUSINESS EDUCATION						
12	102	SPANISH 2	3	D				
20	201	COMPOSITION 2	3	C				
25	103	INTRO TO SPEECH	3	B				
53	114	COLL ALG BUS APPLIC	3	W				
91	221	PRIN ACCOUNTING 1	3	W				
R	81	BUS*BUSINESS EDUCATION						
05	228	GYMNASTICS	1	A				
27	115	CINEMA APPRECIATION	3	C				
45	211	PRIN SOCIOLOGY	3	D				
50	101	GENERAL BIOLOGY 1	CR	E				
53	101	FUND OF MATH 1	3	C				

IESTER	SEMESTER TOTALS				CUMULATIVE TOTALS				NOTES
	COMPUTED HOURS	EARNED HOURS	QUALITY POINTS	AVERAGE	COMPUTED HOURS	EARNED HOURS	QUALITY POINTS	AVERAGE	
79	12	9	18.00	1.50	9	9	18.00	2.00	
80	9	9	18.00	2.00	18	18	36.00	2.00	
80	9	9	18.00	2.00	27	27	54.00	2.00	
81	13	10	19.00	1.46	40	37	73.00	1.83	

TRANSCRIPT NOT VALID WI
SIGNATURE AND TRI-COLOI

ATTORNEY OR PARTY WITHOUT ATTORNEY *(Name and Address)*:   TELEPHONE NO.:   FOR COURT USE ONLY

ATTORNEY FOR *(Name)*: Petitioner In Pro Per

SUPERIOR COURT OF CALIFORNIA, COUNTY OF   LOS ANGELES

STREET ADDRESS: 111 North Hill Street
MAILING ADDRESS: same
CITY AND ZIP CODE: LOS ANGELES, CALIFORNIA 90012
BRANCH NAME: CENTRAL

MARRIAGE OF

PETITIONER:

RESPONDENT:

FILED
LOS ANGELES SUPERIOR COURT

JUL 7 1998

JOHN A. CLARKE

CASE NUMBER:

BD269041

JUDGMENT

[XX] Dissolution   [ ] Legal separation   [ ] Nullity
[ ] Status only
[ ] Reserving jurisdiction over termination of marital status
Date marital status ends: 06-11-98

1. This proceeding was heard as follows: [ ] default or uncontested   [ ] by declaration under Civil Code, § 4511   [X] contested
   a. Date: 06/11/98   Dept.: 7   Rm.:
   b. Judge *(name)*: Hon. AVIVA K. BOBB   [ ] Temporary Judge
   c. [X] Petitioner present in court   [ ] Attorney present in court *(name)*:
   d. [X] Respondent present in court   [ ] Attorney present in court *(name)*:
   e. [ ] Claimant present in court *(name)*:   [ ] Attorney present in court *(name)*:
2. The court acquired jurisdiction of the respondent on *(date)*: 11/03/97
   [X] Respondent was served with process.   [X] Respondent appeared.

3. THE COURT ORDERS, GOOD CAUSE APPEARING:
   a. [X] Judgment of dissolution be entered. Marital status is terminated and the parties are restored to the status of unmarried persons
       (1) [X] on the following date *(specify)*: 06/11/98
       (2) [ ] on a date to be determined on noticed motion of either party or on stipulation.
   b. [ ] Judgment of legal separation be entered.
   c. [ ] Judgment of nullity be entered. The parties are declared to be unmarried persons on the ground of *(specify)*:
   d. [ ] Wife's former name be restored *(specify)*:
   e. [ ] This judgment shall be entered nunc pro tunc as of *(date)*:
   f. [ ] Jurisdiction is reserved over all other issues and all present orders remain in effect except as provided below.
   g. [X] Other *(specify)*:   See attached Pages.

   h. Jurisdiction is reserved to make other orders necessary to carry out this judgment.

Date:

JUDGE OF THE SUPERIOR COURT

4. Number of additional pages attached: 2   [XX] Signature follows last attachment

NOTICE

Please review your will, insurance policies, retirement benefit plans, credit cards, other credit accounts and credit reports, and other matters you may want to change in view of the dissolution or annulment of your marriage, or your legal separation.

A debt or obligation may be assigned to one party as part of the division of property and debts, but if that party does not pay the debt or obligation, the creditor may be able to collect from the other party.

An earnings assignment will automatically be issued if child support, family support, or spousal support is ordered.

Form Adopted by Rule 1287
Judicial Council of California
1287 (Rev. January 1, 1995)

JUDGMENT
(Family Law)

Family Code §§ 2340, 2343, 2346

761551N2

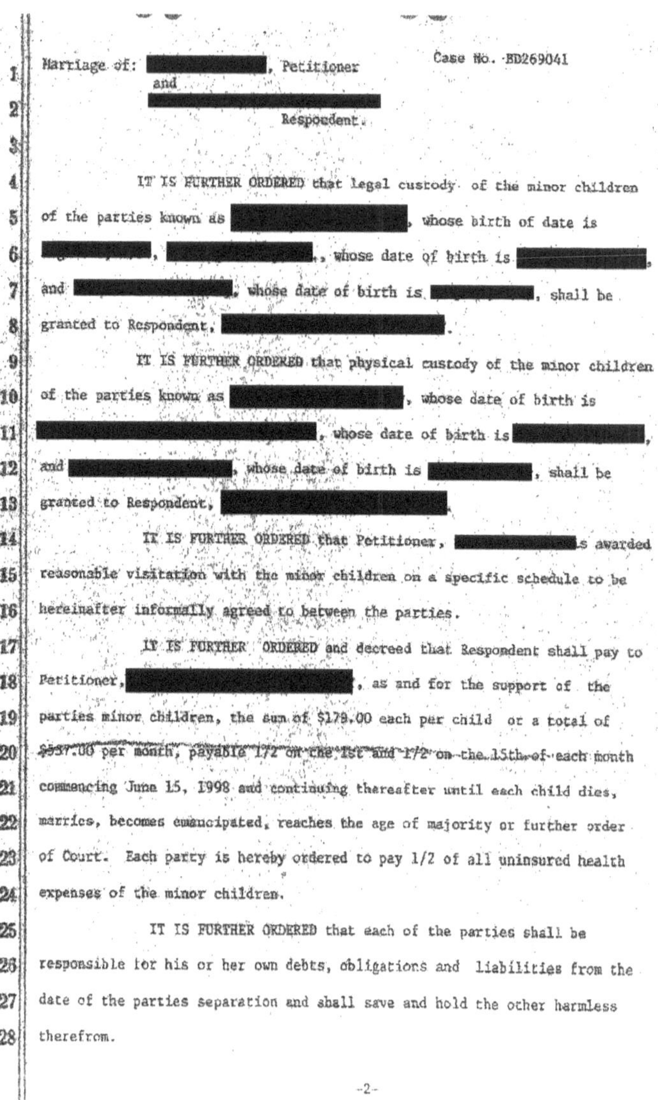

Marriage of: ▆▆▆▆▆▆▆, Petitioner   Case No. BD269041
and ▆▆▆▆▆▆▆▆▆▆▆
Respondent.

IT IS FURTHER ORDERED that legal custody of the minor children of the parties known as ▆▆▆▆▆▆▆▆▆, whose birth of date is ▆▆▆▆▆, ▆▆▆▆▆▆▆▆, whose date of birth is ▆▆▆▆▆▆, and ▆▆▆▆▆▆▆▆, whose date of birth is ▆▆▆▆▆, shall be granted to Respondent, ▆▆▆▆▆▆▆▆▆.

IT IS FURTHER ORDERED that physical custody of the minor children of the parties known as ▆▆▆▆▆▆▆, whose date of birth is ▆▆▆▆▆▆▆▆▆▆▆, whose date of birth is ▆▆▆▆▆▆, and ▆▆▆▆▆▆, whose date of birth is ▆▆▆▆▆, shall be granted to Respondent, ▆▆▆▆▆▆▆▆.

IT IS FURTHER ORDERED that Petitioner, ▆▆▆▆▆▆▆s awarded reasonable visitation with the minor children on a specific schedule to be hereinafter informally agreed to between the parties.

IT IS FURTHER ORDERED and decreed that Respondent shall pay to Petitioner, ▆▆▆▆▆▆▆▆▆▆, as and for the support of the parties minor children, the sum of $179.00 each per child or a total of $537.00 per month, payable 1/2 on the 1st and 1/2 on the 15th of each month commencing June 15, 1998 and continuing thereafter until each child dies, marries, becomes emancipated, reaches the age of majority or further order of Court. Each party is hereby ordered to pay 1/2 of all uninsured health expenses of the minor children.

IT IS FURTHER ORDERED that each of the parties shall be responsible for his or her own debts, obligations and liabilities from the date of the parties separation and shall save and hold the other harmless therefrom.

-2-

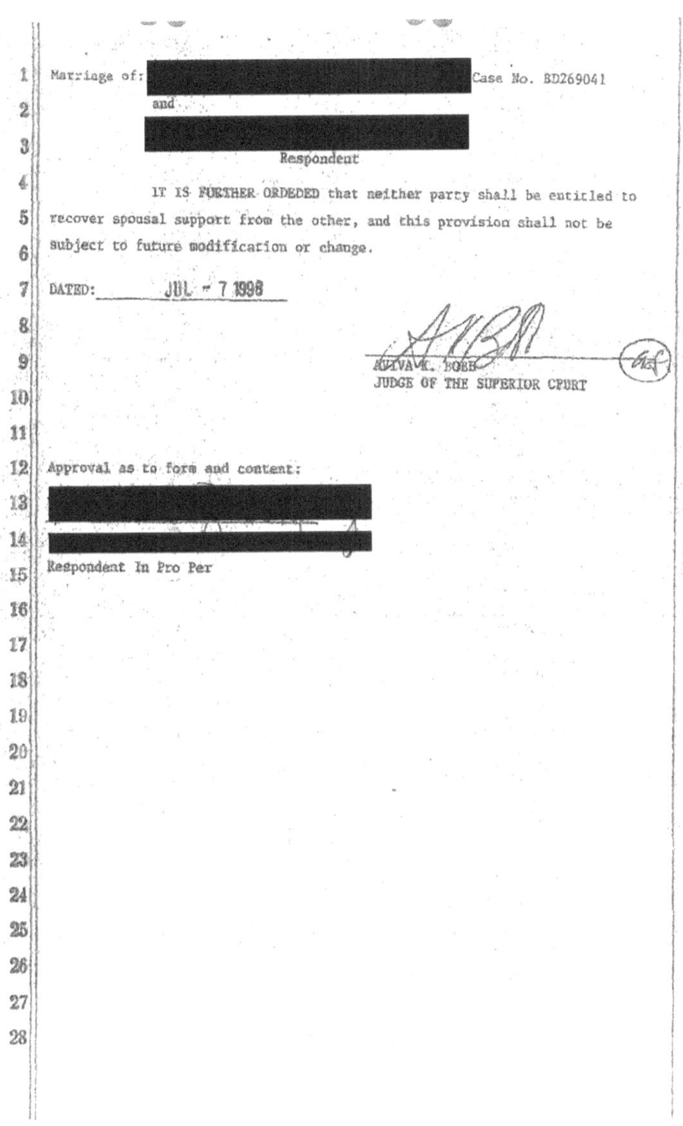

Marriage of:

and

Respondent

Case No. BD269041

IT IS FURTHER ORDEDED that neither party shall be entitled to recover spousal support from the other, and this provision shall not be subject to future modification or change.

DATED: JUL - 7 1998

AVIVA K. BOBB
JUDGE OF THE SUPERIOR COURT

Approval as to form and content:

Respondent In Pro Per

STANLEY MASSEY

Closing

My intention for writing this book is to encourage anyone who is going through the struggle of life. To give you hope when you feel that all hope has been lost. To motivate you not to give up on the people who are dear to you. Now, at age 50, I have found that hope in family who accepted me in my worst condition, at the bottom of life's struggle. It was there that I discovered love. It was there where I saw God, for God is love.

The End

REFERENCES

Alcoholics Anonymous, published by A.A. World Service, Inc. New York, NY. pp. 59-60. (Need to ask permission)

The Holy Bible published by Oxford University Press New York Inc. I John pp. 1324 chapter 4 verse 8.